Supplement Marketing Secrets

How to DOUBLE the Profits
of Any Supplement Business
in the Next 6 to 12 Months

Doberman Dan

Supplement Marketing Secrets

Copyright © 2016 Doberman Dan
ISBN-13: 978-1537177755
ISBN-10: 1537177753

All rights reserved. No part of this book may be reproduced in any form without permission in writing from the author.

This book is for entertainment and education purposes only. The views expressed are those of the author. The reader is responsible for his or her own actions. Adherence to all applicable laws and regulations, including international, federal, state, and local governing professional licensing, business practices, advertising, and all other aspects of doing business in the United States, Canada, or any other jurisdiction is the sole responsibility of the purchaser or reader. Neither the author nor the publisher assumes any responsibility or liability whatsoever on the behalf of the purchaser or reader of these materials.

All images are copyrighted by the author.

Book layout & ebook conversion by manuscript2ebook.com

Chapter 1 - How To Get a 1,183% Return On Your Marketing Dollars. . . . 1

Chapter 2 - This is Where The Big Money is Hiding 13

Chapter 3 - The Master Success Formula. 35

Chapter 4 - You Gotta Get 'Em To Stick. 47

Chapter 5 - The Sales-Boosting Cashflow Surge System. 75

Chapter 6 - The ONLY Way Left For The Little Guy To Get Rich 117

Chapter 7 - How To Create Customers For Life. 141

Chapter 8 - The Highest ROI Activity You Can Invest In 159

Chapter 9 - Your "Print Money at Will" Machine 169

About the Author. 179

CHAPTER 1

I **love** a big back end.

No, not **that** kind of "back end," you pervert. I'm talking about the back end in your business—ongoing sales to current customers.

(Well, now that I think about it, I actually *do* like the other type of big and healthy back end.)

But let's talk about **your** back end.

I'd bet you dollars to donuts it's not anywhere near as big as it **could** be ... especially if you're only working it online.

Or worse yet, not working it at all.

You'd be amazed at how many business owners don't work their back end. Contrary to what they believe, they don't have a "business." They have a moneymaking scheme with a revolving front door.

Dumb, dumb, dumb.

It's easy to tell who these business owners are. They're constantly saying ...

"I need more customers!"

They **think** they need more customers. But getting more customers without an effective back end marketing system is just going to make them go broke faster.

Getting customers nowadays is **expensive** . . . and getting more expensive every day.

So before you invest any more time and money in your front end, you need to do something very important. In fact, if you **don't** do this, you'll be throwing all your advertising dollars down a black hole and slowly going broke.

So here's what you need to do right **now**: Get rid of that revolving door and **keep** the customers you already have.

What you **really** need is a successful and proven system for getting more and more **ongoing** purchases . . . and **bigger** purchases . . . and more **frequent** purchases . . . from all those customers coming in your front door. And I'm going to share a few ideas with you to help you do that.

In my more than 22 years in direct marketing, I can count on one hand (and still have fingers left over) the number of companies who excel at working their back end. And that's a sin... because the most difficult and expensive thing you can do in business is . . .

Get a New Customer!

And sadly, with most businesses, that's where the relationship ends. Oh sure, they might send some emails or add the customer to a half-assed auto-responder sequence . . . but that is no longer an effective way to exclusively work your back end. If that's all you do, you're probably missing out on as much as 50% (or **more**) of the money you **could** be making.

A couple of years ago I had a guy wining and dining me, hoping I would accept him as a client. (I didn't.)

When it came to "bottom line" time, I stared into his beady little bloodshot eyes with my piercing baby blues . . . and presented my advance fee and royalty.

After nearly choking on his Chivas and tonic, he stammered, *"That's eight times more than my marketing director's monthly salary!"*

To which I replied in a calm, slow, and deliberate voice I used to use to subdue unruly drunks back in my cop days . . .

"I realize that's more than you probably pay anybody in your employ, Mr. Slightly Inebriated Guy Who Desperately Wants to Be My Client.

But . . . your marketing manager has no clue whatsoever about . . .

"How to Get a Customer!"

And I do.

And without **somebody** *knowing how to get a customer, there's no reason for the marketing director's job . . . or* ***your*** *position as the owner . . . to even exist.*

And **that** *is why you'll gladly pay me eight times more than you pay your marketing manager.*

But don't worry. We'll keep this our little secret."

Would you like to know why I ended up turning down a five-figure advance and ongoing royalties?

It's simple.

It was painfully obvious this guy just didn't "get it." (Ya know . . . some people are successful **despite** themselves.) He was letting a literal **fortune** (seven figures) slip through his fingers because of his half-assed approach to back end marketing.

When I told him how to quickly fix the problem, he started whining and making excuses. Now I can't stand a whiner . . . so our relationship would have soured very quickly.

And . . . since my compensation was based on performance, he would have cheated me out of a lot of money . . . because he's too stupid or lazy (or both) to properly work his back end.

It's much easier (and a lot less stressful) to start one of my famous KTBs (kitchen table businesses) than to try and drag some clueless client kicking and screaming to success.

Enough bitching about clients. Instead, let's talk about a way you can build a nice, big healthy back end . . . and . . .

Make a Lot Of Money . . .
Month after Month . . .
Year after Year!

When I first launched my newsletter, I made a special charter subscription offer exclusively to my online subscribers. One of the extra unadvertised bonuses that charter subscribers received was a big leather bag. There's an interesting story behind that bag. It has made me a lot of money . . . and can do the same for you, too.

Here's the dealio:

A few months ago I was planning a back end promotion for my bodybuilding supplements business. And I was being my typical cheapskate self, trying to figure out how to save a few pennies here and there on the mailing costs.

Then I had an epiphany.

I had invested a minimum of $40 . . . and as much as $110 to get these customers. Why in the world was I trying to "cheap out" on this back end promotion? Instead, how about I make it as **valuable** as possible . . . even if it bumps up the cost a bit?

And how about instead of just blanket sending it to everybody, I pull out the most responsive customers . . . the ones most likely to buy

… and overwhelm them with a promotion that will not only show my appreciation … but "shock and awe" them, too.

So off I went in search of the perfect grabber … and I found that nice big leather bag here:

http://www.ckbproducts.com

I thought it was fairly classy-looking with a suggested retail price of $44.95. But in quantities of 10 or more, my wholesale price was only …

A Measly 12 Bucks and Change!

I wanted the bag and sales letter to arrive with as much "theater" as I could reasonably afford … so a big old FedEx box was my preferred choice.

Unfortunately, FedEx didn't fit my budget … but a big red, white and blue USPS Priority Mail box **did**. Sure, probably not as much impact and "theater" as a FedEx delivery … but a fairly good option nonetheless. Especially considering this big Priority Mail box was going to arrive completely unexpected.

Response was awesome. The customers were blown away. Many called us in disbelief. Never in their entire lives had a company sent such a nice gift completely out of the blue.

My little campaign accomplished its goal …

It Totally Shocked My Customers and Left Them in Complete Awe of My Little Company!

So instead of "cheaping out," I sent out a back end promotion that not only **appeared** valuable (and got a 100% open rate) … it actually **was** valuable.

It felt really good to do this ... but altruism doesn't pay the bills, does it? I live in the **real** world and have bills to pay and bad habits to support ... like sleeping indoors and eating. So what **really** matters is ...

How Much Money Did This Bad Mamma Jamma Bring In?

Well first, let's break down the costs to get this puppy in the mail:

- Leather bag—$12.65 each
- Priority Mail—$10.50 each
- Sales letter—approx. .75 each
- Fulfillment costs—approx. $1 each

Grand Total: $24.90 Each

I admit, that's a fairly good chunk of change for a mailing ... but I was relatively sure it was going to pay off.

Yes, of course a big Priority Mail box arriving with an expensive-looking leather bag and personalized sales letter was a big part of its success ... but the **real** secret of success for any direct mail promotion is always ...

The List!

I did some fairly meticulous list segmentation to ensure I was only mailing to my very best and most responsive customers.

I've got a friend who can perform all kinds of really complicated stuff I call "list voodoo." And when it's all said and done, he'll provide you with a smoking hot list of starving buyers just **begging** to give you money.

His name is Ben Morris and you can find him at kristalytics.com. The things he can do with list analysis, selection, and segmentation are nothing short of pure magic. If you want the maximum possible results from your direct mail, Ben is "da man!"

If I were mailing a larger quantity I definitely would have contacted Ben. But since this was my first little test of a "shock and awe" campaign, I took my kitchen table commando approach and did the list segmentation myself.

Here's how I did it:

I selected a list of customers who had purchased a minimum of $1,500 over the past five months. I removed all the customers who had done returns or were, according to my fulfillment center, "a pain in the ass." I called the resulting list . . .

My "Whale" List!

It was a little over 200 names . . . with approximately 30% of those international.

International shipping charges were $45/box . . . so I wasn't too comfortable spending that much to mail the international folks and dealing with all the customs issues, too . . . so I removed them from the list.

That left me with a list of about 130 or so "whales" in the United States.

I have to be honest, initial response to the continuity offer was lower than I expected. Don't get me wrong . . . 11.5% response is fairly darn good . . . but I was expecting more. (What can I say? I'm an incurable optimist.)

It initially converted 15 people into a $200/month continuity program . . . and brought in an **additional** $8,100 in other non-continuity back end sales.

I probably could have doubled these results with a few extra tweaks and steps:

Doberman Dan

1. I think assigning a deadline date in the letter would have bumped up response ...

2. A "SECOND NOTICE" and "FINAL NOTICE" mailing spread approx. 14 days apart would have brought in a lot more "on the fence" customers ...

3. And last but not least, a nice little friendly "nudge" by phone would have brought in more people too.

In addition to the big leather bag, the customer received a personalized handwritten letter on cream-colored, monarch-sized paper from the owner/spokesman. Here's what the handwritten letter looked like:

> **From The Desk Of**
> **Rick Gray**
>
> DEAR «Firstname»,
>
> I REALLY APPRECIATE YOU!
>
> I PROBABLY DON'T TELL YOU "THANK YOU" OFTEN ENOUGH... SO I'M SENDING A LITTLE GIFT TO SHOW MY GRATITUDE. I HOPE YOU LIKE IT.
>
> I'M ALSO ENCLOSING A SPECIAL OFFER JUST FOR YOU... MY CREAM OF THE CROP "GOLD" CUSTOMER.
>
> IN THE ATTACHED LETTER I'VE PUT TOGETHER A SPECIAL DEAL... THE MOST EFFECTIVE STACK I'VE EVER OFFERED... AT THE LOWEST PRICE I'VE EVER OFFERED.
>
> IT'S ONE MORE WAY OF SHOWING YOU HOW MUCH I APPRECIATE YOUR SUPPORT.
>
> AGAIN, FROM THE BOTTOM OF MY HEART... THANK YOU!
>
> ALL THE BEST,
> Rick Gray

This was paper clipped to the top of a personalized sales letter written by me. Here's the first page of the letter:

> # <<Firstname>>, Will You Join My Exclusive "Gold" Customer Club And Accept These Massive Savings And Discounts?
>
> Dear <<Firstname>>,
>
> To thank you for being such a loyal customer ... *and* ... because you've <u>proven</u> *beyond a shadow of a doubt* that you're seriously committed to your physique and fitness goals ... I want to offer you an exclusive invitation to join my Gold Customer Insiders Club!
>
> As a member of this **invitation-only** insiders club, you're entitled to benefits other guys will never have access to! Plus, you're going to save big each and every month on all the legal gear you're already using. And last, but certainly not least, I'm offering my own personal time and attention to help you in as many ways possible to reach your goals.
>
> Let me show you *exactly* what's included in your membership to the Gold Customer Club each and every month:
>
> *Membership Benefit #1:*
> **You Get My Most <u>Potent</u> Anabolic Stack**
> **5 Of My Most Hardcore Supplements!**
> *(A $254.75 Value!)*
>
> Each and every month, I'm going to ship you my most potent muscle building, strength enhancing, fat-shredding stack (that I personally use!). Here's what you get:
>
> **Stack Component #1: 1 Bottle Of Hyper Gain Each Month!** Our flagship *Kre-Alkalyn* creatine plus synergistic testosterone boosting compound formula that helps you build *rapid muscle mass and strength!*
>
> Chances are, you're already familiar with the amazing effects of Hyper Gain, but just to refresh:

When it was all said and done, two people dropped out of the continuity program after the first two months. One more dropped out after three months ... but 12 have stuck for six months so far.

That's not just luck, by the way. That's good marketing.

Getting them to stick as long as possible was carefully engineered into this thing from the very beginning.

So let's add up what we've gotten so far from just the continuity income:

- 15 customers x $200/month for 2 months = **$6,000**
- 13 customers x $200/month for 1 month = **$2,600**
- 12 customers x $200/month for 3 months = **$7,200**

Now if every single customer drops out tomorrow (which is highly unlikely) the continuity income so far has generated $15,800.

Add to that the $8,100 in additional non-continuity sales and this promotion so far has generated . . .

A Grand Total of $23,900!

That means if everybody drops out of the continuity tomorrow . . . this promotion has brought in a . . .

738% Return on Investment!

Based on the buying behavior of these customers . . . and all the other cool things I put in place to make 'em stick . . . I fully expect them to stay in this program at **least** another six months.

So let's do the numbers on that:

. . . 12 customers x $200/month x 6 months = $14,400.

Add that to the $23,900 already generated and we get **a grand total of $38,300!**

Hmmmm... glancing down at the calculator in that annoying device that vexes me on an almost hourly basis (the iPhone) I see that turns out to be a whopping . . .

1,183% Return on Investment!

Gee, do you know any other place you can invest your money and get **that** kind of return?

I sure don't.

And that's just one of the many reasons I never put any money into the stock market. My ROI there is basically a crapshoot because I have **zero** control over other people's businesses. But I have a **lot** of control in my own business . . . and therefore a much better potential ROI.

Like I said, there were a couple of other low cost steps I **should** have added to the sequence that I believe would have at least **doubled** the results.

And . . . after seeing these results, I should have **immediately** been on the phone with Ben Morris to have him find more whale customers so I could start rolling this out . . . and making obscene amounts of money. But I seem to follow the Gary Halbert school of direct response testing. I develop new projects and promotions, test them, get spectacular results . . . and then . . .

I Promptly Abandon Them!

Stupid, right?

Maybe. Maybe not. You see, money is no longer my primary motivator. Lifestyle and projects I'm passionate about are what turns me on.

Hey, I've given you several killer ideas that can quickly fatten up that neglected back end of yours . . . and stuff your pockets full of all the cashola your greedy little heart desires.

If you can't make some major moolah with this, you're beyond all hope . . . and I predict an endless series of paper hats and nametags in your future.

CHAPTER 2

I'm trying to help you extract as much business as possible from your past customers and existing flow of new customers and prospects ... because there's a gold mine there.

Most people are leaving a potential fortune on the table every month they **could** be mining from their existing and "lost" customers.

See, most people just focus on getting new customers ... but that's the most expensive and least profitable thing you can do. By spending most of your time and money on that exclusively, you're letting a lot of potential profit slip through your fingers.

Here are just a few back end marketing ideas that can significantly bump up LCV (lifetime customer value) and net profits:

- Just small increases in transaction amount, transaction frequency and the amount of time customers "stick" can result in huge increases in net profit.
- No matter how many you're sending now, you need to send more back end promotions. (Almost nobody contacts their customers often enough.)

- List segmentation—you can communicate more often with your best customers. They want to spend more money with you if you'll provide them the opportunity to do that. And you do that with more frequent "touches" and promotions and offers specifically for the "whale" customers.
- Customer reactivation—offer some kind of discount coupon or coupon for something FREE. The more recent expires should be the most responsive.
- Discover what the buying cycle is for your particular products and services and increase the frequency of communication as they get closer to the beginning of the cycle.

These are all topics to which an entire chapter could be devoted. I just threw those out there to get you thinking about them. We'll talk about all of them in much more detail soon.

I'm trying to get it through your thick head that . . .

The Big Money Is in the Back End!

That realization is what took me from doing just OK to consistently making the big bucks. And I'm gonna keep repeating it until you finally get it.

The caffeine from my Cuban coffee chased with a large cup of Colombian coffee (kinda like a shot and a beer) is **really** kicking in now. If you thought I was bouncing around before, hold on to your hat.

Moving onward in our mission to make you lots of cashola, let's talk about something everybody seems to obsess about . . . but almost nobody gets right . . .

Response Percentages!

Let me tell you something I've hardly ever heard any other marketers reveal . . .

I Don't Give a Rat's Pitootie about Response Percentages!

I love seeing these rookie copywriters bragging about getting really high response percentages. They think they're promoting themselves but they're actually just exposing how clueless they really are.

But first, another little side trip:

Most direct mail copywriters wound up becoming copywriters after a very long and arduous process of learning their craft.

If they endured through that lonely process, most usually were good enough to get the attention of an experienced copywriter, and were given the opportunity to "copy cub" or mentor under a master copywriter.

Many, like me, slugged it out for years, learning by doing it on their own . . . struggling and failing time after time.

In my case, I invested eight long years learning on my own, investing my own money, starting, and testing various mail order projects. I never even **considered** working for a client and risking his money until I had honed my chops by putting my own money on the line.

As opposed to most copywriters nowadays who take a four to six-week course and proclaim themselves to be a top gun copywriter for hire.

Look, I have no respect for any copywriter who hasn't at least once invested his own money writing copy for his own project and making it a success. Only **then** can you consider yourself worthy to accept a client's money, in my most humble (but accurate) opinion.

So if clueless rookie copywriters bragging about their alleged 40%, 50%, or 60% response rates impresses you, let me tell you about a piece I wrote that got a ...

100% Response!

Fairly impressive, huh? Well hold your horses there, cowboy. Let me tell you the **whole** story.

I mailed a lead generation letter (dollar bill letter) to two prospects I was interested in bringing on as clients. (By the way, it's not that hard to get a high response from a lead gen piece.) Both of them contacted me by phone almost immediately.

I had exciting conversations with them about all the great stuff we would do together. I was already counting the money in my head.

Here's what happened to the "hot" prospects from my 100% response lead gen piece:

Just a few years earlier Prospect #1 was hailed as the boy wonder of international finance. Turns out he was running a huge pyramid scheme and was arrested and went to federal prison a short time after our conversation.

When I followed up on Prospect #2 a few weeks later, I discovered he had been fired.

So guess how much money I made from my 100% response?

None ... Nada ... Zero ... Zip!
A Big Fat Goose Egg!

Actually, I was in the negative. Yes, I lost a few bucks, but I lost something much more valuable than money ... my time.

So my 100% response rate isn't that impressive after all, is it?

You see, response rate is not a metric you should be focusing on. The most important thing is . . .

Return on Investment!

Sorry to pick on the bricks and mortar (B&M) folks, but they can be the worst offenders. They'll put a coupon in the Val Pak and then bitch about the low response.

The most important factor in the success of any direct mail promotion is who receives the message.

And Val Pak goes out to everybody in a zip code. How targeted is **that**?

(Plus most Val Pak ads are horrendous . . . the equivalent of a business card—name, address, and phone. No offer, no nothing.)

But Val Pak can still be a profitable part of your customer acquisition, if you don't obsess about response rates and instead focus on your ROI.

If the Val Pak goes out to 10,000 homes, most business owners expect to get a couple of hundred prospects coming in the door. Ain't gonna happen.

Let's say you only get two people to come in and only one becomes a customer. Well, depending on what you invested in the Val Pak mailing and your average unit of sale, you might already have a decent ROI.

A cosmetic dentist who invests $1,000 in Val Pak and has an AUS (average unit of sale) of $4,000 has already made a 400% ROI, based on this example.

Do you think he should be bitching about a .02% response . . . or jumping up and down about a 400% ROI?

Duh!

So forget response rates. Instead, let's focus on ways we can bump up your ROI from your advertising.

In Chapter 1, I shared a case study of one of my back end promotions that brought in a 1,138% ROI. That's a great template for you to follow ... but let's go over some ways you can bump up the ROI even more from promotions like that:

1. Select the customers from your list from whom you're most likely to get the best response. (I told you a quick and easy way to do that in the last chapter.)
2. Find an eye-catching grabber that fits your budget. A dollar bill is always a good one ... but if that's too rich for your blood, check out 3dmailresults.com. They have a bunch of cool doo-dads you can get cheap ... some for only a few pennies.
3. Create a unique way to tie your message in with the grabber.
4. For best delivery and open rates, hand-address your envelopes and send them 1st class with a live stamp, not a printed indicia.
5. Put a deadline for ordering in your sales letter. Make the deadline approximately 5 to 6 weeks from the date you'll drop your mail.
6. Approximately 12 days after you drop the first mailing, remove all the people from the list who have purchased and send a "SECOND NOTICE" mailing to those who haven't yet purchased. I like to put this on the top of the letter:

SECOND NOTICE

That's one of many handwritten graphics you can get from Mike Capuzzi at copydoodles.com.

I also like to use a different grabber on this second mailing. You'll need to change the opening so it jives with this new grabber.

Want a good grabber idea for this "SECOND NOTICE" mailing? Those little plastic bugs with googly eyes at 3dmailresults.com are cheap, they make your envelope "lumpy" and you can open your letter like this:

Dear Friend,

I don't want to "bug" you, but since I haven't heard from you yet, I wanted to make sure the letter I sent a couple of weeks ago with the dollar bill attached didn't accidentally slip past your attention.

Alrighty then.

The next step is the one I always have to fight people to do. But if you'll listen to me and actually do it, you'll probably **double** your sales from this whole dealy-bop.

7. Call the prospects who haven't bought yet and ask them for an order. Here's a sample script:

Hi, Joe Prospect? This is Richard Cranium.

I'm the guy who sent you the letter with the dollar bill attached a couple weeks ago . . . and the letter with the googly-eyed bug a couple days ago.

Did you get those letters?

Have you had a chance to read them yet?

Was there anything you had any questions about?

May I ask your help with something?

I'm trying to get some ideas to improve my marketing and customer service.

Do you mind me asking why you didn't order after getting my letters?

Those questions are going to give you some incredibly valuable marketing intel. I know from personal experience big direct marketing companies, like Rodale, Phillips, and Agora, have invested **millions** to get this type of information. You're going to get it for the price of a phone call.

And you'll get more sales too.

I think I know what's going through your mind right now.

I spent a few years in belly-to-belly and phone sales. The reason I started my first mail-order business was to get **away** from that stuff. If you don't know what you're doing, it can be absolutely brutal.

So I can appreciate your reluctance about doing this step. If you stick to the script I gave you, it really won't be all that bad. Most of your customers will be receptive to your call. Your letters have already "greased the skids" for it . . . so it won't be a cold call. In many cases, it will be that last little gentle nudge they need to buy from you.

Yes, I appreciate the fact you got into direct response and online marketing so you **don't** have to make phone calls . . . but to double your sales from promotions like this, it really is worth doing.

If you absolutely can't stand the thought of doing it, hire a skilled salesperson to do it for you, and pay them a commission on each order.

It's a quick and simple way to significantly bump up ROI from these back end campaigns.

Wanna Peek Over My Shoulder?

Speaking of ROI, would you like to look over my shoulder and see a little project I'm working on today?

You might find it helpful to get a brief peek inside my demented brain and see how I figure out where to invest my money for the greatest ROI.

Here's the dealio:

The owner of the lettershop I use contacted me a few days ago to tell me he found 4,900 mail pieces of mine in inventory he didn't know he had. I'd totally forgotten about them too. They were from a promotion I did over a year ago.

This is a common occurrence. I'm always juggling too many projects and things sometimes get lost or pushed to the back burner.

(Some sharp PWM could probably make a fortune by following me around for a few months and implementing all the successful tests and projects I come up with.)

Anyhoo ... I paid for these booklets a while ago, so all I'd have to invest now would be the lettershop services and postage. It's kinda like a little found opportunity to make a little money on some neglected leads.

Soooo ... the first thing I do is open up my handy dandy little direct mail spreadsheet. Yes, the very same one I will give you as a shameless bribe when you subscribe to my humble little publication.

I want to see if it makes sense to invest my money in this mailing ... versus blowing it on women and booze.

Actually, what I'd **really** rather spend it on is gold, silver, some ridiculously expensive guitar, or a handmade boutique guitar amplifier.

Any of those choices would be much better than leaving it in worthless fiat Federal Reserve notes held hostage in a collapsing banking system.

But I digest.

Now never mind that I haven't showered since my half-hour walk this morning. Lean in close, look over my shoulder, and take a look at this. (Don't let a little BO keep you from making a lot of money.)

A	B	C
	Direct Marketing Analysis	
(Use this spreadsheet to determine if a direct mail campaign can be profitable for a specific product. Enter data in column B only. Results shown in column C)		
Gross Margin per Unit		
Selling Price	$120.00	
Add: Handling Charge	$24.00	
Total Revenue per Unit		$144.00
Cost of Merchandise	$15.00	
Shipping or Delivery	$15.00	
Order Processing	$9.00	
Cost of Returns	$0.00	
Bad Debt	$0.00	
Other	$0.00	
Total Cost per Unit		$39.00
Gross Margin per Unit		$105.00

Here's how I arrived at these numbers:

I took a "worst case scenario" approach (always a good idea) to see if this is worth doing ... or if I should start looking for the next guitar to blow my money on instead.

- The mail piece pitches a $40 monthly continuity product. In this example I'm assuming the customer only sticks in the auto-ship for three months. (Actually on average it's longer than that ... but we're planning on a worst-case scenario, remember?)

  So $40 x 3 months = $120.

- The handling charge the customer pays is based on three months' worth.

  $8 shipping and handling x 3 months = $24.

- Our product cost is a little less than $5 a bottle, so

  $5 x 3 months = $15 product costs.

- The next line "Shipping or Delivery" is what we pay to ship the product. That's approx. $5 ... so

  $5 x 3 months = $15.

- "Order Processing" is what we have to pay the fulfillment company to stuff the product and "swag" into an envelope or box. That's about

  $3 x 3 months = $9.

So our total cost for getting those products to the customer over that three-month period is **$39**.

That leaves us a **gross margin or contribution to overhead per customer of $105**.

OK, now that your nose is accustomed to my BO, lean in close again and check this out:

Supplement Marketing Secrets

Description	Qty	Cost	Estimated Total:
Run data through National Change Of Address Database and update customer address list with move data	0.5	100.00	50.00
Ink Jet address and Order # directly onto 6x9	4,900	0.0275	134.75
Manual Inserting	4,900	0.04	196.00
Machine sealing	4,900	0.01	49.00
Adding Zip Plus 4 & Barcodes to data, Removing Duplicates from List, Sorting, Bundling, Sacking or Traying, Preparation of Paperwork, Delivery to the Post Office	4,900	0.03	147.00
Subtotal			576.75
3rd Class Postage, Letter (up to 3.3oz)	4,900	0.27	1,323.00

This is the quote from the lettershop, *U.S. Mailing House*, showing the breakdown of the costs to mail the remaining 4,900 booklets.

So back to our handy-dandy spreadsheet (that some wickedly cool guy was nice enough to give you) and let's enter this info in the "Direct Mail Cost per Unit" section.

Direct Mail Cost per Unit	
Circulars	$0.00
Letters	0.00
Inserts	0.00
Lift Pieces	0.00
Envelopes	0.00
Order Forms	0.00
List Rental	0.00
Assembly	0.04
Addressing	0.03
Postage	0.27
Other	0.04
Direct Mail Cost per Unit	**$0.38**

There aren't specific spots in the spreadsheet for certain things like machine sealing, adding zip plus and bar codes, so I combined them in the "Other" cell.

One important thing not included is the printing cost of the booklet. If memory serves me, I paid around .75/each for these. Since I already paid for them, I'm considering it a free gift from the mail order gods and haven't included it in our mailing costs.

Let's take a look at my projected worst-case scenario of 1% response.

I know I'm repeating myself... and I'm gonna keep repeating it until I pound it into your head...

I Don't Give a Rip about Response Rates!

It can be .00000000001% for all I care. The only thing I care about is return on investment.

I usually get higher than 1% response from back end promotions so this is a fairly low-ball guess.

Net Profit and Break-even Point		
Units Mailed	4,900	
Response Rate	1.00%	
Unit Sales		49
Gross Margin		$5,145
Mailing Costs		$1,850
Fixed Costs		
Creative Development	$50	
Allocations, Other	1	
Total Fixed Costs		$51
Total Net Profit		$3,244
Sales required to break even		1
Mailing needed to break even		76

As you can see, when it's all said and done, even with a lower than average (for me) response rate, we'll still get a 175% ROI from this little promotion.

Not bad.

But I think I can do better.

Let's see how much more we'll make if I get a 2% response... which is still really conservative for this particular little biz.

Supplement Marketing Secrets

Net Profit and Break-even Point		
Units Mailed	4,900	
Response Rate	2.00%	
Unit Sales		98
Gross Margin		$10,290
Mailing Costs		$1,850
Fixed Costs		
Creative Development	$50	
Allocations, Other	1	
Total Fixed Costs		$51
Total Net Profit		$8,389
Sales required to break even		1
Mailling needed to break even		30

Now we're talkin'. Would you be happy with a 453% ROI in the stock market? If you did that consistently, you'd be considered a financial genius and the talk of Wall Street.

Just for fun, let's see how much we could enrich our coffers (and how many guitars I could buy) if we did a little better.

Net Profit and Break-even Point		
Units Mailed	4,900	
Response Rate	5.00%	
Unit Sales		245
Gross Margin		$25,725
Mailing Costs		$1,850
Fixed Costs		
Creative Development	$50	
Allocations, Other	1	
Total Fixed Costs		$51
Total Net Profit		$23,824
Sales required to break even		1
Mailling needed to break even		10

Golly gee whiz whillikers! Other than buying a kilo of cocaine, cutting it with baby laxative, turning it into crack and selling it rock by rock, where else in this crazy world can you get a 1,287% return on your money so quickly?

(By the way, the cocaine selling deal carries a lot more risk than my little direct mail plan . . . so don't even **think** about it.)

Wanna hear something absolutely crazy that might completely blow your mind? (That'd be a small explosion, wouldn't it?)

In the very recent past, I've gotten an **11% response** from this exact same promotion.

Again, since we don't really care about response rates, what that means is a **2,956% ROI from our little $1,850 investment** . . . and . . .

A Whopping $54,694 Smackeroos in Our Pocket!

Are you starting to see how this direct response stuff is supposed to work?

If you've followed the advice of clueless marketing people, you probably have a "revolving door" business . . . and you're totally missing out on the really big money you **could** be making.

Wanna take a quick look at this little booklet that's gonna let me indulge in my favorite vices? (No, not **that**. My motto is . . . one woman, many guitars!)

The first obstacle you have to overcome to make a sale with email and direct mail is you must . . .

Get Your Message Opened!

Here's one effective way to do that:

It's scaled down here but it's a 6x9 envelope. I used a 6x9 for a couple reasons. First of all, that's the size of the booklet. (Duh!) But also, because I've discovered many times a 6x9 gets a higher open rate than a plain old #10 envelope.

I've included some teaser copy to make it look like the prospect is receiving a book they ordered. Kinda sneaky? Yeah, I guess so ... but they really **did** order the previous book. And this is an important follow-up to that ... so I still consider it part of their original order.

Whatever. Nobody has ever complained ... and it gets me a really good open rate and ROI.

Here's the cover and first inside page of the booklet:

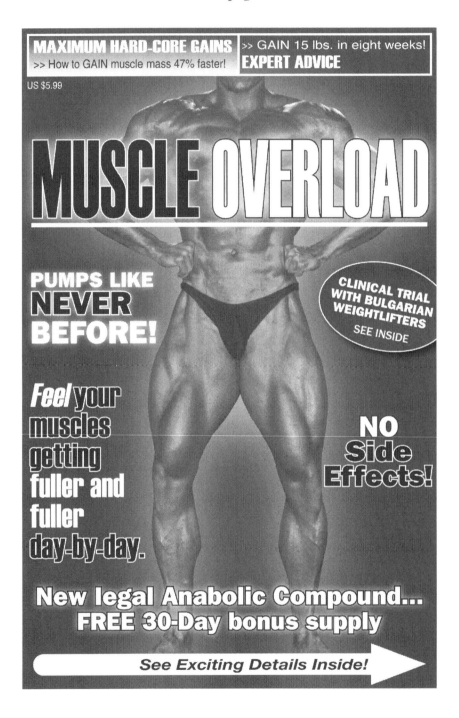

Here's how to make even BETTER and FASTER gains with *Muscle Overload Training*

Dear Friend,

A few weeks ago you requested my free book, *Muscle Overload Training*.

If you follow the training and nutrition advice exactly as revealed in the book you can make some really fast gains in muscle size.

But I've discovered a secret that will help you gain muscle even FASTER.

And that's exactly what I'm going to reveal in this special report.

So read on to discover a GUARANTEED way to gain muscle mass 47% faster with *Muscle Overload Training*...

Sincerely,

Rick Gray

Rick Gray

The first page reminds them they ordered Rick Gray's free booklet recently and tells them why they're getting this second one.

This little test should be interesting since many of these leads are fairly old . . . but I think it's worth a try since the printing was already paid for.

If I can make this work to these cold leads, I've got another 25,000 or so I can mail. It'll be like getting a nice big influx of new customers without kissing Google and Bing's big boo-tays.

(Don't ask why these leads were allowed to go cold. I'd like to point the finger at somebody else . . . but there would be three pointing right back at me. Hey, nobody's perfect.)

"Hey, DD . . . Have You Thought about Switching to Decaf?"

Yes, I realize I jumped around a lot in this chapter. I had a lot I wanted to share with you . . . and I wanted to get it all said.

There is a method to my madness. I'm revealing the stuff you can do right away that will have the biggest and fastest impact on your bottom line.

I realize some of this stuff might seem fairly basic to my "big boy" players . . . and that reminds me of another story about my copywriting mentor.

A few years ago, Gary Halbert was at a seminar where Ed Mayer was teaching two different sessions on direct mail . . . beginning and advanced.

If you've never heard of Ed Mayer, he was known as "The Dean of Direct Mail." He was the undisputed expert at the time, having performed conversion "miracles" for some of the biggest and most successful direct mailers in the world.

Halbert could only attend one of Ed Mayer's sessions ... so would you like to guess which one he chose?

The Beginner's Session!

Halbert was asked why somebody with 40+ years' experience in direct mail and had written the most widely mailed sales letter in history would choose to attend the beginner's session.

He replied:

"If I'm missing something ... or screwing anything up ... it's almost always something basic I've forgotten or neglected. I need to constantly refresh my knowledge of the basics."

If one of the most successful marketers in history knew this to be true, what makes you think you are any different?

We All Need to Constantly Stay Grounded in the Basics!

That's what the most successful marketers, copywriters, and entrepreneurs do ... and that's why they're so successful.

Rookies think they need the fancy, new BSO (bright shiny object) flavor-of-the-month "marketing breakthrough."

The pros know there's no such animal.

To some, it might appear I'm just giving you the "simple stuff." But trust me ... I really do have a plan. You see, all results are based on one thing and one thing only:

Action!

And I want you taking action on the stuff that works.

But ... if you're not gonna take action on the tried and true basics ... what's going to happen when I give you the advanced stuff?

You **still** won't take action ... and you'll just be more confused.

Don't worry though ... it's coming. As soon as you're ready for it.

Before we can have an intelligent conversation about calculus, you need to understand 2+2=4.

Capiche?

Now quit wasting all your time and money on that "revolving door" of yours and go mail and email something to all those customers you've been ignoring.

But, before you go, one more thing ...

I still get a kick out of being called a "guru."

I don't consider myself a guru because I know the **real** reason I've been successful. I'm just a guy who kept missing his target time after time after time ... but kept on shooting.

I got into the mail order business back in 1994. And I started marketing **real** products (not ebooks) on the Internet to **real** people in **real** markets (not the scammy "make money on the Internet" niche) way back in 1996.

Truth be told, 9 out of every 10 things I've tried didn't work. But I just kept trying. I don't know if that's how one becomes a "guru" but that was (and still is) my formula for success.

Most direct marketers and online marketers have a high failure rate. Even huge companies like Agora, Phillips, Rodale, etc., who have more money than **God**, usually only have 3 successful projects out of every 10 they launch.

The odds are usually **worse** for "kitchen table commandos" like us'ns.

But don't get discouraged. In the next chapters, I'm going to show you how to greatly improve those odds. You're going to discover some of my most jealously guarded secrets you can use to increase your success record by ...

At Least 100%!

You're going to discover why most marketers have such a high failure rate . . . and the five specific things you can do to increase your chances of success . . . without risking even one red cent.

You see, one of the biggest secrets to success is knowing how to identify and choose winning markets . . . but most online marketers totally screw this up.

I'm going to reveal the four types of markets and their odds of success.

I'll then show you how to easily analyze the market potential for your idea, product, or service. You'll **immediately** know whether you have a realistic chance of stuffing your pockets with all the cashola your greedy little heart desires . . . or if you'll bomb completely, leaving you broke, depressed, and in the fetal position, sobbing and sucking your thumb.

These are some high-level "playa" secrets you can't get **anywhere** else . . . and can't afford to miss.

You should really check out all the marketing secrets I reveal for free online. I'm quite humbled that my list of online followers is growing by leaps and bounds. There are more than 200 articles about how to increase your sales and profits here:

http://DobermanDan.com

CHAPTER 3

After going broke (again), homeless, and living in my car at the end of 2005, I decided to do whatever it took to make a lot of money fast ... so (hopefully) I'd never have to be in that position again.

After coming up with a new product and sales copy, my initial testing (financed with the last few hundred dollars' credit on my Visa) revealed I had a winner. I immediately started implementing what I call my ...

Master Success Formula!

I'm amazed how few business owners understand this secret ... especially online business owners. When you totally "get it" and implement this in your business, you're going to see some fairly meteoric growth.

Conversely, you're going to struggle a lot and constantly have a "revolving door" business if you **don't** understand this formula. (Ask me how I know.)

The Master Success Formula is the quickest way to boost profits 100% to 800% . . . or more. And, as you're going to see from my real-world example, 100% to 800% increases are conservative . . . because this formula works like crazy. If you understand it and do it, you can create . . .

Quantum Leap Growth in Your Business and Enormous Increases in Your Income!

Before we get into the details of the Master Success Formula, let's talk about a very common problem that stops many people from taking action. I'm talking about the overabundance of marketing information available today. It seems like every month some guru has a product launch pitching a brand new whiz-bang technique . . . or the latest and greatest technological breakthrough for getting more customers. (Most of that stuff is complete BS. There really aren't any new formulas or techniques for getting customers and sales.)

But when that crap gets thrown at you every month, it's easy to get sidetracked by all the different ideas and theories. And *that* causes . . .

Overwhelm and Confusion!

Which stops progress dead in its tracks.

So please allow me to cut through all that crap flooding your mind and make this as brain-dead simple as possible . . . so you can overcome your feelings of confusion and overwhelm, start taking action and moving forward again.

There are only three ways to build your business:

1. Get more customers . . .
2. Get more purchases from each customer . . .
3. Get bigger purchases from each customer.

See. I **told** you it was simple!

You might even be thinking, *Well geez, that's really obvious. I've heard that before.*

Oh really? If you already know it, why aren't you doing it, Einstein?

Don't tell me. I already know the answer.

You've been chasing the BSO (bright shiny object) solution to all your marketing problems. If you've fallen victim to that mindset, you're probably operating from false information you got from some Internet marketing guru. You've never been counseled by somebody who operates **real** businesses . . . in **real** markets . . . selling **real** products.

Instead, you've sought advice from guys whose only gig is being a guru . . . and selling downloadable BSO products to their blind and deluded followers. If these guys had to make it in a **real** consumer market, most wouldn't survive 30 days.

And *that* bad information has you doing what 95% of business owners do . . .

Constantly chasing more and more new customers . . . and completely ignoring the most profitable part of your business . . .

The Back End!

I can't even begin to tell you what a monumentally huge mistake that is. You're literally letting a fortune slip through your fingers . . . month after month.

Again, ask me how I know. My first five years as a rookie mail order business owner, 90% to 95% of my marketing budget (money **and** time) was spent on getting new customers. I mostly did like everybody else and ignored my back end.

When my back was against the wall and the wolf at the door, I finally sent a direct mail letter to my most recent thousand customers. After analyzing the results of that, I finally came to the realization I had let a minimum of $500,000 in back end sales slip through my fingers during the previous five years.

Yeah . . . I left a half a **million** dollars on the table because of my stupidity.

I don't want to see you do the same . . . so pay attention. As you're soon going to see, you can totally transform your business into a money-generating machine . . . in only a matter of months. What I'm about to share will literally take **years** off your learning curve to building a highly profitable business and . . . if you want . . . building a multimillion dollar business.

The first category in our formula is . . .

Get More Customers!

It amuses me that most business owners spend a majority of their time, money, and energy on this first category. In fact, for most businesses, that's all they **ever** do . . . and it's the most expensive marketing you can possibly do. There's little or zero profit for you in this category. If you're lucky, you'll break even. In most cases, you'll probably go negative.

Let me explain.

Let's say it costs you $50 in advertising costs to get a new customer . . . and your customer acquisition offer has a $40 profit. That means you just lost $10 to get a new customer. So how in the world are you going to make money doing **that**?

It's called the "back end," my friend. (Hey, that rhymes! I'm a poet . . . and was not even aware of that particular fact.)

This is where category #2 and #3 of the Master Success Formula come into play. Let's look at what would happen if, instead of just focusing on getting new customers, you spent equal amounts of time, money, and energy on categories #2 and #3 . . . get more purchases and get bigger purchases?

What do you think would happen? I'll answer that for you because I've witnessed the results firsthand. You'd experience a **quantum leap** in income. Your income might jump up so fast it just might scare you. (It did me.)

I'm going to show you a real-life example in just a second . . . but for now let's go over a couple of hypothetical examples to show you the power of the Master Success Formula.

Let's say you have 300 customers who purchase an average of $30/month from you. They actively purchase this amount for six months. This can either be a continuity program or a customer who buys from you and continues to buy additional products on the back end. So you have 300 customers spending $30/month for six months. That's total revenues of $54,000.

Get More Customers	Get More Purchases	Get Bigger Purchases	Total Revenues
300 customers	6 months	$30/month	$54,000

Let's say during the next year you decide to increase each of these three categories by only 33%. That sounds doable, doesn't it? You're going to get 33% more customers, 33% more purchases from those customers . . . and 33% bigger purchases.

Let's see what that looks like . . .

Get More Customers	Get More Purchases	Get Bigger Purchases	Total Revenues
400 customers	8 months	$40/month	$128,000

That's a 237% increase in sales. Nothing to sneeze at, is it?

Let's take this one step further. What would happen if you **doubled** the results of all three categories in the original example I showed you?

Now you have 600 clients who purchase $60/month from you for 12 months.

Get More Customers	Get More Purchases	Get Bigger Purchases	Total Revenues
600 customers	12 months	$60/month	$432,000

That's an **800% increase** in sales! And that, my dear reader, is a lot more cashola for you.

Here's a real-life example. I did an article at DobermanDan.com titled "1300% Increase in Sales in 5 Months." That article wasn't about the how-to of the Master Success Formula . . . it was about all the challenges the business owner experienced with that kind of extremely rapid growth. It was an article to let you know that one day, God willing, you'll experience that kind of rapid growth. And, if you'll learn from that experience, you'll be prepared for some of the challenges that come along with it.

I have a confession about that blog post. I talked about my client and all the exciting things that happened to him as a result of his rapid growth. Well, let me tell you something about that client I **didn't** reveal.

This particular client is the biggest pain in the ass I've ever had to deal with. He makes the most unreasonable demands on me . . . and many times I find myself working day and night for this whip-cracker.

In case you haven't figured it out yet . . .

The Client Was Me!

You see, I was doing some freelance work back then and I came to the same conclusion as many other freelance copywriters . . .

Clients Suck!

Actually, many of my past clients are "salt of the earth people." They have been some of the sharpest marketers and entrepreneurs I've ever met. I now consider most of them friends and confidantes and my life is better for having known them.

In reality, only about 10% of the few clients I've worked with sucked. And of those, only two were filthy, lying, larcenous scumbags who stole from me. (They're now "sleeping with the fishes.")

Seriously though, in the entire scheme of things that ain't bad odds.

Client work isn't really a terrible gig, but I decided to buy my freedom and focus on a little side business I had at the time ... instead of being stuck in the "freelance spiral" constantly getting sidetracked from my own projects by more and more client work.

At first, while I was still doing client work, I only worked on this little business a couple of hours a week. Some months the sales were $2,000 ... some months $5,000. The average monthly sales were anywhere from $2,000 to $5,000, depending on a few factors. The most important being how much I personally focused on it. (Amazing, isn't it? The more I focused on it, the more money it made. Novel concept, huh?)

After deciding to fire all my clients, in November and December 2005 I started testing some new things. After those tests I knew I had a tiger by the tail ... and could make a small fortune if I wanted.

January 2006 I started rolling out. Check out what happened. Here's a screen shot from my 1shoppingcart account:

Sales Reports: Monthly Sales Totals

Date From 1/1/2005 Date To 5/31/2006

Month	Orders Count	Gross Sales	Net Sales
January 2005	43	$5622.85	$5235.85
February 2005	27	$3529.55	$3217.55
March 2005	19	$2118.35	$1908.35
April 2005	19	$2467.10	$2198.10
May 2005	36	$4476.80	$3966.80
June 2005	45	$5534.25	$4835.25
July 2005	33	$3596.70	$3211.70
August 2005	76	$6887.60	$5956.60
September 2005	106	$8886.80	$7701.80
October 2005	108	$9921.40	$8722.40
November 2005	98	$6381.20	$5377.20
December 2005	107	$7724.50	$6627.50
January 2006	197	$8172.15	$6089.30
February 2006	682	$23695.90	$16061.55
March 2006	1069	$42581.15	$30714.30
April 2006	1529	$62111.95	$44610.15
May 2006	1383	$70664.20	$54927.20
Grand Total	**5577**	**$274372.45**	**$211361.60**

Record Count:17

Would you like to know how I did that? It's simple. I implemented the Master Success Formula I've been sharing with you ... and I took ...

Massive Action!

I tested everything before I started rolling out, but once I had things in place that were working, I rolled out in every available media I could.

Doesn't that just make sense? When you have a promotion that's kicking ass, why would you want to severely repress your results by limiting yourself to only one media? (Online marketers, listen up.) Not only do you leave 50% or more of your potential income on the table month after month, you're building your business on a foundation of shifting sand. Many of those things you're doing online (SEO, Google AdWords, Bing

PPC, etc.) will be pulled out from under you . . . overnight . . . with no notice.

It's not a question of **if** it will happen . . . more than 20 years of online marketing history prove it's a matter of when.

I'll never understand why so many online marketers keep making the same mistakes . . . and keep getting the rug pulled out from under them time after time . . . after time.

Bottom line . . . when you're dependent on only one media, you are **constantly** at risk of being put out of business in a New York minute. If I were you, I wouldn't rest until you get a **stable** of media working for you so you minimize this risk.

Look, I've made enough mistakes to last three lifetimes. You can be smart and learn from my mistakes . . . and the overwhelming historical evidence. Or . . . you can choose to make the same mistakes yourself . . . and learn the hard and expensive way like I did.

The pastor's sermon has concluded. Please drop your tithe in the offering basket on your way out of the sanctuary. ☺

OK, let's get back to work.

Here are some of the things I did to get that rapid growth after my initial testing:

1. **Google AdWords** for front end business.

2. **I also had an eight-week customer retention autoresponder** series follow-up for the people who bought my front end product. (It was a continuity product . . . so I did everything I knew at the time to get them to stick as long as possible.)

3. **I rolled out in most of the magazines** in the bodybuilding niche. I rolled out two types of ads . . . fractional page lead-generation and also full-page ads that went directly for a sale. The lead-gen and full-page ads went slightly negative . . . but I **more** than made up for it on the back end.

The lead gen ads were quarter page ads. Most of the ad was devoted to a headline like this:

"FREE Report Reveals yadda yadda yadda . . ."

The call to action was "Call toll-free, 24-hour recorded message for more information." When the prospect called and left their name and address, we sent them the product information via snail mail.

Here's something interesting I discovered from previous testing in the magazines . . .

When I've tested a call to action driving people to an opt-in website vs. calling a toll-free number to request a free report in hard copy via snail mail, I converted almost 50% more of the snail mail prospects. *And . . .* they had a higher lifetime customer value than the customers I got by driving them to an opt-in website.

That little test saved and made me quite a bit of money . . . without investing any more money on advertising. That little discovery was a doozy for me.

WARNING: Be careful you don't step in *anybody's* dogma . . . including mine. This is what *my* testing revealed in *my* business back in 2006. That doesn't necessarily mean that's how it's gonna work out today in **your** business. There's only one way to know for sure . . .

Test, Test, Test!

Alrighty then. Moving on . . .

4. **I also sent back end offers via direct mail.**

This caused the biggest cash flow infusion and the biggest increase in sales.

Until that point, most back end offers my customers received were sent via email, which, for a lot of reasons, is not a good idea. I'm not saying to **not** send offers via email. I'm saying it's a bad idea to rely on email *exclusively* for sales messages and customer communication.

Why? I've said it before and I'll continue saying it until the situation improves . . . if it **ever** improves . . .

Email Deliverability Sucks!

Your customers' in-boxes are flooded with worthless time-sucking emails every minute of every day. They're overwhelmed and have to deal with it by deleting them en masse . . . unopened. Unfortunately, the reality is . . . only about 25% of your emails are even getting through to your customers because of ISP spam filters, people deleting them unread . . . and God knows what other glitches. People nowadays are even deleting stuff unread they signed up for and *want* to read . . . because of in-box overwhelm. That includes *your* messages too.

If you're OK with low open rates and response (and getting worse) because it's relatively hassle-free, then by all means, stick with email only. Some people prefer convenience to maximum ROI. I didn't understand that before . . . but I do now.

But . . . if you want maximum response and maximum ROI from the investment of time and money in your business, you should really be sending back end offers via direct mail.

If you do it like I do it, you're going to have *ridiculously* higher deliverability rates, open rates and response (and cashola!) than you get from email. And **that** is why I use direct mail for back end sales.

5. **I also used direct mail for customer acquisition.**

The ads working well online and in the magazines were formatted into a direct mail piece. I mailed that piece to the only list available of bodybuilding product buyers. It's a small niche so there are very, very few direct mail lists available for rent. Usually none.

Truth be told, that sole bodybuilding list didn't work out too well for me. It was almost completely dead from neglect. The data card information from the list owner was not accurate. It hadn't been maintained or mailed in years ... yet they represented it as updated and current.

Here's a little tip that can save or make you a lot of money: The more often you direct mail a list, the more responsive it becomes. If you **don't** mail a customer list regularly, (once a month is probably close to ideal) it starts to die a little bit every month. After a year or so, it's almost completely dead.

So in the bodybuilding niche, customer acquisition direct mail isn't really an option. But if you're working in a niche that has a fair amount of lists available, direct mail customer acquisition is definitely an option you should test.

6. **I implemented an upsell after the initial order.**

The customer was presented with an upsell offer approximately double the cost of the front end product. If they ordered online, the upsell was presented online. If they called in to order, the customer service rep presented the upsell after securing the initial order.

I got approximately 20% of the customers taking this initial upsell offer. That's a lot of money I would have left on the table had I not offered it.

7. **I implemented several "stick" strategies.**

This is a multimillion-dollar lesson in and of itself. Imagine **doubling** your lifetime customer value with very little increase in marketing costs.

Getting new customers is the most expensive and least profitable thing you can do. Without these stick strategies your business is stuck in "revolving door" mode and you're letting a lot of money slip through your fingers.

And *that* is something we'll have to talk about in the next chapter. I promise it will be worth the wait.

CHAPTER 4

In the last chapter we discussed the Master Success Formula. You now understand that making maximum money from your business is really quite simple, isn't it? But we left off with the thing that can make the biggest impact for your bottom line ...

Stick Strategies!

Stick strategies are designed to make your customers "stick" longer ... in other words, stay active longer, buy more products, refer more people, etc. If you have any kind of continuity or auto-ship programs (and you should), you can probably **double** your retention with a well-executed stick program.

What I'm going to share helped me take a floundering supplement auto-ship program from a pathetic one-month (or less) average stick rate ... to four to five months.

And that made a HUGE difference in my bottom line. You see, doubling stick rates doesn't just double your net ...

It Causes EXPONENTIAL Increases in Profits!

It's like money for nothin' . . . and your checks for free. Why? You get three times . . . five times . . . or ten times+ more purchases from your customers . . . by only investing a tiny fraction of what you invested to get those customers in the first place. And that sure beats the typical revolving door most businesses are stuck in . . . constantly chasing more and more customers on the front end without maximizing the value from the customers they already have.

So allow me to share more about how I took my little hobby-level side business, generating a very modest part-time income, to a nice little cash cow, generating a very high five-figure monthly income . . . in only five months. By the way, about three months after that, this little KTB (kitchen table business) was into six figures a month . . . and heading toward a $5-million/year business. That is, if I hadn't slammed the brakes on and took two years off. But that's a story for another time.

Anyhoo . . . at first, my front end for this little KTB had the customers paying only shipping and handling for their initial bottle . . . then they were enrolled in a discounted monthly continuity program. It was done completely ethically, unlike many of the forced continuity offers you see today. Many hide the fact that it's a continuity offer and do sneaky things with their terms and conditions . . . like hide them in tiny 4-point gray font that looks like this: (_{4-point gray font}).

Before my customers could place an order, they had to confirm two separate times they understood it was a monthly auto-ship. The terms were very explicit. Post-order they also got an email confirmation message reiterating the terms . . . and the same message in hard copy was sent with their initial order.

The monthly continuity was one of the biggest reasons for the rapid growth of this KTB. With continuity income you don't have to start all over again on the first of every month. You've got some steady income you can count on.

That's all well and good when you can get people to stick . . . but I was only keeping people on my auto-ship approximately one month. Totally defeats the purpose of an auto-ship, huh? It was so exciting to see big numbers coming into the auto-ship program . . . and so depressing to see them drop out just as quickly. The average supplement industry "stick rate" for continuity is three months . . . and even though that seems low to me, I wasn't even close to average. I quickly discovered if I didn't implement a stick strategy, my customers weren't going to stick around very long at all. Sticking just one month was only enough to cover my customer acquisition costs. If I wanted to make some profit, I needed to keep them longer.

Here's how I initially did that:

Instead of just a mundane supplement auto-ship, I positioned this deal as an exclusive "preferred customer membership" that included a subscription to my preferred customer newsletter, *The Hardcore Training Journal*. It was not an email or online newsletter. It was sent every month in hard copy via the good old-fashioned US Postal Service. I was already delivering an email newsletter and online articles to these customers but neither had any effect whatsoever on my stick rates. I hoped the offline newsletter would. *The Hardcore Training Journal* included really good training and nutrition info every month and a discount coupon code the customer could use on other products. I also usually included a separate insert with a product offer. And what a coinkydink . . . the discount coupon code in the newsletter was for the product offered in the insert.

I did **not** just send the newsletter along with their monthly continuity product . . . for a very good reason. Based on my experience, the more you keep yourself in your customers' top-of-mind awareness with lots of regular and frequent contacts, the more their lifetime customer value increases.

To be totally honest, at first I resisted doing all this. It was added expense and I didn't want to write another newsletter. But it sure was worth it because...

My Auto-Ship Retention More Than QUADRUPLED!

These auto-ship customers are your best customers and you need to communicate with them frequently. With this customer "stick" newsletter, your monthly direct mail back end offers and the monthly continuity product, they're receiving some kind of communication from you **in hard copy** three different times each month. When you add in your email newsletters, online articles, and email offers, they might be hearing from you six or more times per month. And usually, the more "touches" they get, the more money you make.

(By the way, wanna add one more "touch" that can *significantly* boost lifetime customer value? Call them on the phone once a month.)

OK...I'll admit it...I'm kinda lazy. And these stick strategies created more work for me. So to save time and money, I tried to do away with the hard-copy newsletter. I tried replacing it with an eZine. Stick rates plummeted...and people got really pissed off. I also tried to replace it with a membership site where they could go download a PDF newsletter formatted exactly like the hard-copy newsletter. Again, stick rates went down the crapper and I had a whole bunch of pissed-off customers.

None of the digital delivery stuff I tried worked to increase retention. The only thing that worked was sending the newsletter in hard copy. So yeah, it created a little more work...but it took a continuity program that was a revolving door with very little profit...to an *obscenely* profitable dealy-bop with a **much** higher lifetime customer value.

Why did it only work in hard copy? I can only guess. Probably because stuff delivered via email or online has very little perceived value...and the online methods have a pathetically low delivery and open rate. Frankly, I didn't worry about *why* it worked . . . I just knew it worked and put a LOT more cashola in my pockets. Without these stick methods I would have just been spinning my wheels . . . and doing a lot of work for a tiny profit.

A word of warning: If you're doing any kind of free trial offer like this . . .

Keep a close watch on your "mooch" factor!

I was a featured speaker at my mentor Gary Halbert's Root Canal seminar in Orlando, Florida, in 2005 when he said something really important that went over most attendees' heads:

"People on the Internet are cheap bastards!"

Halbert . . . what an eloquent wordsmith. But that little utterance has stuck with me all these years . . . and has made me a **lot** of cashola.

Your "mooch factor" is all those cheap bastards who only want something free and have no intention whatsoever of buying anything. They come out of the woodwork in droves when you offer any kind of free trial online.

My mooch factor in that market was about 50%. In other words, half the people who got the free bottle either cancelled their auto-ship before the first month even kicked in. Or 30 days later, after the first auto-ship order was charged, they'd cancel their auto-ship and request a refund. The really low-life scumbags would do a chargeback. My numbers and cash flow couldn't support that. There are some markets that are so big you still might be able to make money with a mooch factor as high as 90%. I couldn't . . . so I changed my initial offer so the customer actually has to cough up cash on the initial order.

That mostly cut the mooch factor down to zero. It suppressed response quite a bit too. Cut it by about 50%. But the 50% I lost was mostly the moochers who never bought anything on the back end . . . so this new offer started bringing a much higher-quality customer who stuck on the auto-ship longer. So, interestingly enough, by suppressing response with the new offer, marketing and fulfillment costs went down, back end sales went up and . . .

Net Profits Increased Exponentially!

Don't just take my word as the "gospel according to Doberman Dan" and copy what I'm doing . . . because it might be different in your business. But if you're doing any kind of free trials, it's essential you keep an eye on your mooch factor.

Wanna know another easily implemented and inexpensive trick you can use to boost LCV? It's the humble little . . .

Stick Letter!

It's amazing how well these little sap-suckers work.

Why? Actually a couple reasons:

1. The stick letter is actually a sales letter. It sells your customers (again) on why they made the purchase in the first place. It helps reduce buyer's remorse, one of the biggest causes of refunds.
2. It lets the customers know you really care about them and appreciate their business.

You'd be surprised how many business owners take their customers for granted and never properly thank them. When you let your customers know you appreciate them . . . and you do it from the heart . . . it makes a big impact.

It also adds one more "touch" they get from you . . . and the more touches they get from you, the higher your lifetime customer value.

Especially in the "honeymoon" phase . . . the first 90 days of them becoming a customer.

Here's how I do it in my supplement business. First of all, here's the envelope:

Just a plain and simple white #10. I use courier font because it gives it a more personal look. The "VIP Offer Enclosed" teaser is in bright red. It's a Copy Doodle, an awesome collection of sales letter and website graphics offered by my subscriber Mike Cappuzzi at www.copydoodles.com. You should check it out. And the letter:

ANABOLICSECRETS.COM
HARDCORE SUPPLEMENTS

A.S. Research • 384 Green Leaf Drive • Grovetown, GA • 30813
Telephone: 866-869-5392 • E-mail: sales@anabolicsecrets.com

Dear «Firstname»,

As you can see, I've attached a dollar bill to the top of this letter.

Why have I done this? Actually, there are two reasons...

1. I have something <u>extremely important and urgent</u> to tell you... and with all the junk we get in the mail, I needed a unique way to make <u>sure</u> I caught your attention.

2. And... <u>since</u> what I have to share with you is about <u>saving a lot of money</u>, I thought the dollar bill would be an appropriate "eye catcher".

Here's what it's all about:

My name is Rick Gray. Recently you purchased supplements from my website at AnabolicSecrets.com... or maybe requested my FREE book *Muscle Overload Training*... and I wanted to say...

Thank You, «Firstname»!

I really mean it.

You know, it seems to me not enough business owners appreciate their customers. I'm different. I <u>do</u> appreciate my customers. Very, very much.

You may not know it yet, but your decision to become one of my customers is, from a financial point of view, one of the smartest decisions you've ever made.

Why?

Because now that you're a preferred customer, **you're going to get the best deals and biggest discounts** I <u>never</u> make available to the general public.

The very <u>best</u> deals, discounts and special introductory offers of just-released products are **reserved only** for preferred customers like you, «Firstname».

Also enclosed with this letter is <u>another</u> letter that

(Please go to the next page...)

> – Page 2 –
>
> I think will be of great interest to you.
>
> At the beginning of this year I made an incredible offer to a handful of my very best customers. I gave them the opportunity to <u>have me help them personally</u> with their training and diet.
>
> I also gave them **$467.75 worth** of hard-hitting muscle building, fat incinerating products and benefits... at a **killer 60% discount!**
>
> As you can expect, this offer was snatched up faster than you can say "Wow!"
>
> Because this muscle-building/fat-burning special (along with my personal help) was so <u>deeply discounted</u>, I was only able to make it available to a very small, hand-selected group of my very **best** customers.
>
> But since you're a new preferred customer, **I'd like to extend the same offer to you,** «Firstname».
>
> **But You Must Reserve Your Spot Within The Next 7 Days... Or You'll Miss Out On This <u>60% Discount</u>... AND My Personal Guidance!**
>
> If you delay, I'm going to have to cross your name off my list and pass your spot to the next customer in line.
>
> If you're truly serious about making <u>dramatic improvements in your physique</u>, this special offer... and all the bonus gifts... can be the shortcut to <u>finally</u> having the physique you've always dreamed about.
>
> <u>Read the enclosed letter right away</u> so you don't miss out on this amazing opportunity to **get my personal help with your bodybuilding goals.**
>
> I really do appreciate your business, «Firstname». Please don't hesitate to contact me if you ever need anything.
>
> Sincerely,
>
> Rick Gray, President
> A.S. Research
> AnabolicSecrets.com

Pretty underwhelming, huh? Yeah, I admit . . . not really any amazing copywriting and persuasion secrets going on there. Just sincere appreciation and gratefulness . . . and the dollar bill attached to the top gets me a lot of bang for my buck . . . literally!

Doberman Dan

This letter is sent via First-Class Mail® as soon after receiving the order as possible . . . preferably the same day, even before the order is shipped. Definitely no later than the very next day.

Here's why I think this letter is so effective: *Nobody* does anything like this. It hits the customers completely off guard. Sure, they expect you to send the product they ordered . . . but they sure as hell don't expect a personal letter from the owner with a dollar bill, telling them how much he appreciates their business.

How about one more example? (You might remember this one if you're in my *Marketing Camelot* membership.)

Supplement Marketing Secrets

Dear «FirstName»,

I was just outside playing with the dog... and the Colombiana (my wife) shouted, "Amor, «ShipToName» has just been knighted into your Marketing Camelot." So, before I did anything else, I wanted to say...

Thank you, «FirstName»!

I really mean it. You know, it seems to me not enough business owners appreciate their customers. If they do, very few seem to actually express it. I'm different. I do appreciate you. Very, very much.

Look, you made a wise decision to join my Marketing Camelot.

Why?

Simply because it delivers more hardcore, real-world, business building, moneymaking instruction than any other publication or membership on the planet.

In my sales letter I promised to reveal some rather unique ways to make more money and build your business.

Well, keep an eye on your mailbox. Your "new knight" package has been meticulously assembled by squires (assistants to knights) wearing immaculately clean white cotton gloves, carefully packaged and lovingly prepared for shipping. It's on its way to you as we speak.

Thank you for choosing to be knighted into my Marketing Camelot... and welcome to my extended family.

All the best,

Doberman Dan

P.S. I had the squires include a couple little extra unannounced gifts in your new knight package. I hope you like them. Pax vobiscum.

Although none of the colors show up (obviously) in this book, the letter is sent on ivory Monarch stationery with a gold metallic border, in an ivory Monarch envelope with a gold metallic seal. I'm going for a classy VIP look... because that's what you are to me... a VIP.

I've gotten a lot of positive feedback about this letter and I'm flattered that many people are swiping this idea for their own businesses.

How does it work?

Well, I can't point to any hard and fast numbers like I can with the supplemental biz-stick letter . . . but I have an unbelievably high stick rate to my newsletter. So far, I'm eleven months into this little doo-hickey and 88% of the subscribers I launched with are still with me. I can't say the stick letter is responsible for that, but it's definitely a contributing factor.

I think I know what you're thinking right now:

"Can't I just implement these stick strategies with email?"

You probably know I'm a big proponent of separating yourself from the lazy masses and getting better response by going offline, so you might be surprised at my answer.

Yes! That's the beauty of our business. You can choose convenience over maximum ROI. Believe you me . . . I *totally* understand that now. Sometimes making less money but keeping things simple is a good choice, depending on your goals.

But based on my results, email didn't really work . . . even though I had a 12-week follow-up/stick auto-responder sequence. The offline stuff eclipsed it by so much it wasn't even funny.

But really . . . it isn't very expensive to farm this stuff out to a fulfillment company. (I know a couple good ones if you need one.) That way the whole process will be totally on auto-pilot for you. So there! Now you have no excuses.

If you're running a start-up or kitchen table business, you could easily do all this stuff yourself with a computer and cheap printer. That's how we're still doing the stick letters for the DDL . . . in-house using Colombian and Peruvian slave labor. (My wife, the Colombiana, and her friend from Peru.) It really doesn't take that much time to do it for a kitchen table-level business . . . and it pays for itself *many* times over.

The back end is where your fortune is hidden, and it's the easiest and most inexpensive marketing you'll ever do. You're probably leaving a **lot** of money on the table month after month . . . when there are some very simple and inexpensive things you can do to *rapidly* boost customer retention and lifetime customer value. All you have to do is get it started.

And remember . . .

"You don't have to get it perfect . . . you just have to get it going."

~~~

Sooooo . . . how exactly are you going to do all that? Well, one way is with what I like to call my "SBCSS."

Sales-Boosting Cashflow Surge System!

Remember a few years ago when product launches were all the rage in our much maligned (for good reason) and incestuous little Internet marketing niche? The guys selling $2,000+ BSOs (bright shiny objects) made it seem like a big fat discombobulated and complicated process. See, it not only helps justify the high price tag when you make a BSO seem complicated, it also naturally leads to selling the "done for you" service on the back end . . . for a 10x to 100x multiple. (These dudes are smart. You can learn a lot by observing their process of selling these *Online Magic Riches Button That Spits Out $100 Bills* type of products. You'll probably learn more by observing than from the product itself.)

But a product launch process really isn't all that complicated. In fact, in this chapter I'm going to show you part one of my simple little product launch system you can quickly and easily implement for BIG sales and cash-flow surges.

Even more important, once you get my simple product launch process nailed, I'm going to show you how to put it on auto-pilot. **Then you'll have an evergreen moneymaking asset in your business, constantly working for you 24/7 to generate new customers and ongoing back end sales.**

You see, as successful as product launches are for building a list, growing your network of affiliates, and creating big pay days and cash-flow surges, the way most lesser mortal marketers have taught the process has quite a few disadvantages.

Don't get me wrong, you can make a lot of money with product launches, but the disadvantages make it darn near impossible to break free from the grunt work. You can have a good business . . . but you'll be a slave to it.

Why?

- **Launches are dependent on you interacting in "real time" with your customers and affiliate partners.** That's the complete opposite of having what I like to call a "lifestyle business."—a business that allows you a lot of time freedom while still producing dependable and reliable income.

- **Every new launch is a brand new "start from scratch" deal.** You always have to start from zero. And because each new launch is a brand new deal, you can't really tweak, test, and incrementally improve the process like you can with an asset such as a successful direct mail promotion or online marketing funnel.

- **Since each launch is a brand new start-from-zero deal, they're not really predictable, accountable, and reliable, are they?** Basically you don't know the outcome until the fat lady sings. If your launch doesn't go well, you've invested a lot of time, money, and effort for naught.

- **If your launch isn't successful, you probably have a lot of unhappy affiliates.** They've wasted a lot of time and effort . . . with pathetically small commissions . . . or **zero** commissions. Believe you me, it's gonna be a **lot** harder to get these guys and gals to promote your next launch . . . if they promote it at all.

- **When it's over, it's over.** And most of your affiliates probably didn't promote it . . . so you missed out on a lot of new customers and sales. Affiliates have their own schedules and it's arrogant of you to expect them to drop everything else they're doing to promote your launch. This leaves a lot of money on the table that **could** be yours . . . **if** you could get all your affiliates to promote it.

- **Many affiliates won't promote due to "list overlap."** In other words, a lot of prospects in the market are on a lot of different lists. For that reason, your affiliates might not want to mail when everyone else in your niche is mailing. I can't say I blame them either. That always seemed fairly stupid to me.

- **Many affiliates don't want to participate because you can't give them reliable metrics.** (See the "each launch is a brand new start-from-scratch deal" bullet above.)

- **Customer service overload.** Launches can overload your business infrastructure and your support staff. Unless you're really ready for the spikes, your customer service can get overloaded and unable to respond in a timely fashion. When all your hard work pays off and you start getting more customers than ever before, that's a really bad time for your customer service to go to crap.

- **Launches overload *all* aspects of your business** . . . because of all the last minute changes and "improvising" that goes on behind the scenes as you interact with your customers, gather new intelligence based on their feedback . . . and incorporate what your market is telling you. And you're forced to put out all the "fires" you never anticipated.

- **Launches can overwhelm YOU.** You have to be the "general" in charge of the battlefield, giving orders to the troops in response to what's happening in real time. Your troops don't have a set of standard operating procedures for all the stuff that can happen in the heat of battle. Even if they did, they'd probably screw it up.
- **Your business becomes a "one-legged table."** See, one of the biggest keys to a successful product launch is all the affiliate partners promoting for you. Not necessarily a *bad* thing ... but if you become addicted to the "rush" of launches and wind up too dependent on them, you become too dependent on affiliates ... rather than relying on a multitude of marketing channels.
- **You become an "affiliate whore."** To get a decent percentage of affiliates promoting your deal, you've got to constantly kiss butt and schmooze them. When they *do* promote for you, you're now in their debt. Which means you have to promote all of *their* offers to *your* list. Imagine having 50 affiliates who promoted your launch and now you have to promote 50 different affiliate offers to your list. You can almost kiss your schedule for promoting your own products goodbye. Your calendar will be too full promoting all your affiliates' offers. Talk about overloading your list! But if you don't promote their stuff, they'll never promote for you again.
- **If you ain't in the "good ole boyz club" you won't get a big affiliate push.** Almost every niche has its "good ole boy" network. It consists of the big players with the big lists. These guys are already networked and joint venturing with one another. Unless you've got some kind of "in" or close personal connection ... or you're willing to go to the time and expense of schmoozing them to try and get your foot in the door ... it's almost impossible to get the big sales push you need for the huge launch successes you hear about so often. To do the really big numbers, you need the good ole boyz club to promote your launch. And just like the mafia, you're now indebted to them. (See the "affiliate whore" bullet above.)

- **Launches make you a slave to your business.** For all the reasons I've already mentioned, if you allow your business to become reliant on launches, it becomes more reliant on **YOU**. There are so many last minute "seat of the pants" decisions you as the entrepreneur/general have to make in the middle of a launch . . . it's darn near impossible to delegate it to somebody.

Yes, I realize that seems like a lot of negatives, but it ain't *all* bad. I'm just telling you all the possible pitfalls so you can choose to avoid them . . . or step right in them with full knowledge of what you're getting yourself into. You can't say nobody warned you.

I've done really well with product launches . . . but I've done them on my own terms, using my own techniques to limit the negatives. Yes, it limited the potential pay-off too . . . but I'm OK with that. I'd rather make less money than turn myself into a slave to my business, and even worse, an affiliate whore.

If it hasn't sunk into your noggin' yet, know this . . .

Launches Are a Tool in Your Marketing Toolkit . . . NOT a Business!

Many rookies make the same mistake with the Internet. It's not a business . . . it's simply a medium . . . one that should be included with a *mix* of other media if you want a stable, predictable, and reliable business. (You wouldn't sit on a one-legged stool, would you?)

I just want to make sure after you experience success with your first product launch, you don't become overly dependent on them. They should only be a tool in your toolbox. So . . . your Dutch uncle DD is gonna show you a different approach to launches.

A simpler approach.

One that can be implemented quickly. In only a matter of days... instead of weeks or months of preparation needed for the overly complicated launch processes taught to the IM junkies.

Not only do I want to eliminate all the drawbacks of traditional launches, I want you to be able to leverage all your hard work and put everything into an evergreen auto-pilot system to help free you from the grunt work of your business.

Sound like a plan?

Good! Let's get started.

Do you know the #1 thing that will determine the success of your product launch?

The "Who" Behind the Eyeballs Looking at Your Launch Materials!

It all comes down to the list.

And how are you going to make sure the eyeballs looking at your launch process are the ones most interested and most qualified?

List Segmentation!

That's just a fancy way of saying you're going to get the people on your general list to raise their hands and say, *"Yeah I'm interested in that topic. Please send me more info."*

I've discovered building sub-lists is a **HUGE** secret to getting ridiculously high response rates and multiplying your income exponentially. You can do it online and/or offline. For now, let's start with how to do it online. It's really quite simple:

1. Send a fairly blind teaser email to your list to drive them to a squeeze page. The only thing you're "selling" is getting them to the squeeze page. Something like this should work fairly well:

"Hi <firstname>,

If you want a hard body without the hard work, I've discovered something fairly amazing. The experts said you could never get six-pack abs this easy . . . but I've proven them 100% WRONG.

Click here to discover all the exciting details."

2. Once they're on your squeeze page, the only "sale" you need to make is to get them to opt in to the sub-list. If they have the least little bit of interest in your topic, a squeeze page something like this should accomplish that goal.

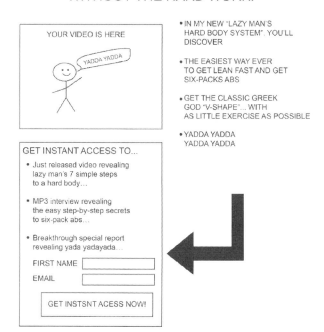

I have to give my friend T.J. Rohleder credit for that killer headline. He showed it to me when I was in Kansas a couple of weeks ago. He got the idea while editing copy for a biz-op offer in front of the TV when one of those fitness infomercials came on. It's brilliant. It's what *everybody* wants . . . regardless of the niche. But if you're in the fitness niche, I believe you could make a lot of plata with that headline.

Anyhoo . . . back to our squeeze page template.

Keep your opt-in box "above the fold" as much as possible. If you can't do that with the style of squeeze page shown, move it to the top right, beside your video. (Once you get this project going there are several variations you should test . . . but that's a topic for another chapter.)

3. Once your prospects have opted in to your sub-list, start the process of "teasing" and building excitement for the launch date. You can do that with a series of videos, audios, PDF reports, emails, or a combination of all four.

Now I'd like to share a little known never-before-revealed (to my knowledge) secret you can use to get . . .

FIVE TIMES More Sales from Your Launch!

For maximum success of your launch, hopefully you'll promote both online and offline. Simply adding some offline promotion to your launch process will boost your response . . . but when you do it like I'm about to show you, it can be a fairly significant boost. It might even eclipse your results from your online stuff.

How much more response can you get from direct mail than the exact same copy sent via email?

A recent article in *Target Marketing* says . . .

> "Mail campaigns draw a better overall response than digital channels. For instance, response rates for direct mail to an

*existing customer average 3.40 percent, compared with 0.12 percent for email, which is roughly a **30-fold difference**."*

I've consistently gotten 200% to 600% higher response in direct mail vs. email . . . *and* a much higher percentage of customers buying the highest-priced options from the direct mail promotion. Which, for the umpteenth time, confirms Gary Halbert's eloquent statement about the difference between online and offline market conditions . . .

"People on the Internet Are Cheap Bastards!"

So why don't more people do direct mail as part of their launch process? No idea. Ignorance, apathy, slothfulness, downright bone-headed stupidity . . . that's my only guess . . . because it ain't any harder than sending email, as you'll soon see.

When doing list segmentation offline, I like to call it "lead generation to your own list." It's a little known secret of the big players that can generate a **lot** of money . . . even from a relatively small house list.

We're gonna keep this brain-dead simple for you to take away *all* your excuses for not doing it and at *least* **DOUBLING** sales from your launch:

1. Take the email copy you used to get people on your sub-list and put it on a canary yellow 4 1/4" x 5 1/2" postcard. Yeah . . . just plain black type on a yellow postcard. No fancy graphic designer needed. The subject line from your email will be your headline . . . and the body copy from the email is the body copy on the postcard.

2. If you want to go to the extra effort and expense of using a PURL (personalized URL) as your response device, go for it. If you were doing lead-gen to a cold list that's probably not a bad idea. But since this is lead-gen to your house list . . . people who already

know, like, and trust you (hopefully) I don't think a PURL is going to boost your response enough to warrant the extra hassle and expense. We're keeping this simple, remember?

3. Take a list of your customers who have purchased from you within the last 30 days, 90 days, 180 days ... or even within the past 12 months ... and send them a simple postcard to drive them to your squeeze page. (Use some kind of tracking so you know which opt-ins came from the postcard promotion and which came from the email promotion.) Your postcard will look something like this:

Your name
106 5th St NE
Barberton, OH 44203

Turn Over to Discover How to Get a Hard Body... without All the Hard Work!

Customer Name

123 N Main St

Flunkytown, OH 44203

How to Get a Hard Body ... Without All the Hard Work!

If you want a hard body without the hard work, I've discovered something Amazing.

The experts said you could never get six-pack abs this easy... but I've proven them 100% WRONG.

Go here now to get your FREE report and discover all the exciting details:

www.HardBodyWithoutHardWork.com

4. Stop worrying. This is all new to you so you're experiencing the wonderful effects of stepping outside your comfort zone. (You should do that more often. Wonderful things happen for the few who regularly do that.) *"But I don't know how to send a postcard! This will cost money in postage and printing! Waaaa, waaaa, waaaa."* Look, sending a simple postcard and even a full multi-component direct mail package is as simple as sending an email. Don't have a cow.

5. All you have to do is send a PDF of your artwork and a .csv or Excel file with your list to a service like click2mail.com or USMailingHouse.com. They handle everything for you. (BTW, I've used both services and can personally vouch for them. Of course, with vendors, things can quickly change, so caveat emptor.)

Don't go getting your panties in a bind about using direct mail, OK? I know you think it's scary because you've never done it before and email is free. ("Free" for those who place no value on their time.) But trust me . . . you can regularly get 2x to 30x more sales from the same promotion sent in direct mail than email.

If it were me, I'd do offline lead-gen to my house list a little differently:

1. I'd still send the postcard, but my response device would be to call a 24-hour recorded message and leave a snail mail address. I'm gonna pitch 'em in direct mail **only** because I get an *infinitely* higher delivery rate, open rate, conversion, and ROI in direct mail.

2. We could really start narrowing our offline list down to some *hyper*-responsive people if we wanted. I would segment out all the known direct mail buyers and only mail my postcard to them. And all the follow-up pieces would go out to them *only* in direct mail. You see, for the most part, people continue buying how

they initially bought. So direct mail buyers are direct mail buyers. Online buyers are online buyers. Knowing that little secret, I want to target my known direct mail buyers how they prefer to buy ... with direct mail. And drive my online buyers to the opt-in page.

But I'm getting a little off track. I'm supposed to be keeping this simple for you 'cuz you're a direct mail virgin and *"you be acting all scared and stuff."* So quit stressing about all this direct mail and have yourself a beer (or two) and relax. Just send an inexpensive and simple postcard like I told you using one of those services to keep it easy on yourself. Don't let me confuse you with all the other cool things I can do to ...

QUINTUPLE Your Return on Investment!

I'm afraid that would make you so much money ... and take you so far outside your comfort zone ... you couldn't handle it. That's why I'm keeping things simple for you. We certainly don't want you making too much money, do we?

Back to our plan.

We're doing email and postcards to get the people most likely to respond to our launch offer to metaphorically raise their hands and get on our sub-list. Once they're on the sub-list, there are endless variations of how you can build excitement for your launch date ... and finally "climax" and open this bad boy up for a **flood** of orders.

But I'm trying to keep this simple to minimize the "confusion and overwhelm, deer-in-the-headlights, frozen with fear, taking no action" reaction so many people experience when they're faced with too many great marketing ideas.

Here is how we're going to build excitement and a "buzz" about our launch. (Building a "buzz" helps get this thing going viral ... your existing customers sharing it with their contacts.)

1. After they opt-in to the sub-list, take them to a *"Congrats, you're in"* page with a countdown timer showing the days, hours, minutes, and seconds left until your launch. These are easy to install. Any halfway competent freelance geek can install one for you.

2. Have an auto-responder message sent immediately, letting them know they're now one of the privileged few on the "inside track." They'll get a jump on all the poor schmucks on the outside who didn't get in and won't find out about this great offer until it's too late . . . and all the lucky insiders have already picked the carcass clean.

3. Have auto-responder message #1 do one of four things:

   A. Directs them to an online video that "teases" and builds excitement about the launch. (The more "blind" the better. In other words . . . don't let the cat out of the bag just yet. Just tease about the benefits and hit on the biggest hot buttons.)

   B. Directs them to an online or downloadable audio recording that does the same thing mentioned in "A" above.

   C. Offers them a download link to a PDF special report that does the same thing mentioned in "A" above.

   D. Gives them a link that directs them to an "online special report" (a webpage, dummy!) that does the same thing mentioned in "A" above.

   All we're doing is priming the pump, getting them excited about the upcoming launch and building a buzz. I've given you four different ways to do that in step three. Pick whichever one you're most comfortable starting with.

4. A couple days later, auto-responder #2 goes out. Same deal as auto-responder #1. Tease, build excitement, fan the flame of that buzz that's starting . . . but don't start lifting your skirt and revealing any leg yet. This is a game of seduction and if we rip off our clothes and shout "take me, you big stud" at this point, we've

ruined the whole deal. Again, choose any of those four options I mentioned above . . . video, audio, PDF report, or online report. They *all* work so just choose whichever one you prefer. Ideally it would be nice if you use a variety of those options for each step in this process . . . but that's not necessary.

5. A couple days later, auto-responder #3 goes out. (By the way, as we get closer to the launch date, the frequency of your messages will increase . . . even to three or four a day on the day of the launch.) Tease, tease, tease. "Teach" them about your amazing new breakthrough product without revealing any "meat." Dan Kennedy is a master at this. Frank Kern is the online master . . . and he learned it from Dan Kennedy.

In other words, we still haven't started lifting our skirt. They can still only see our ankles . . . but they're *imagining* what's north of that. (And in many cases, our prospect's imagination is *much* better than the reality.) We're still just in the flirting stage . . . batting our eyes and playing coy. The only thing we want them to do is go to our page on launch day.

I think I got a little over-ambitious (well, a *lot* over-ambitious) thinking I could cover such an important process in only one chapter. Even though my "SBCSS" is simplified for fast implementation, I can't do it justice in only one chapter. It's just too important for your future to "half ass" it, rush through it, and cheat you out of the millions that could and **should** be yours.

So we're going to continue our discussion of my "SBCSS" in the next chapter. It's gonna get *really* exciting when I show you how to put everything on auto-pilot. Now instead of investing so much time, money, and effort for a one-shot launch and cash-flow surge that's over as fast as it began . . . you'll have an evergreen, predictable, accountable and reliable money-making asset in your business that keeps pumping out new customers and cashola month after month, year after year.

Take a quick break, if you need to, and then come back and let's continue this important part of the process to get you on your way to earning big bucks!

CHAPTER 5

Sales-Boosting Cashflow Surge System!

A brief refresher: Product launches are great for boosts in sales, customer acquisition, and affiliates . . . but once they're over, they're over. All that time, effort, and monetary investment for a one-time shot in the arm . . . then it's right back to the status quo.

But that's not the worst of it. Once entrepreneurs see the big jumps in sales that can happen, many of them get addicted to product launches. They then become dependent on them and no longer have a stable business that can continue without them. They basically allow their business to become a "money-making scheme" that simply goes from product launch to product launch. It's the polar *opposite* of how a successful entrepreneur should arrange his business.

That's why I think you're going to be excited when I show you how to put everything on auto-pilot. Now instead of investing so much time, money, and effort for a one-shot launch and cash-flow surge that's over as fast as it began . . . you'll have an evergreen, predictable, accountable, and reliable money-making *asset* in your business that keeps pumping out new customers and cashola month after month, year after year. But first . . .

A Quick Order of Business . . .

In the last chapter I mentioned that I have used both click2mail.com and USMailingHouse.com for mailing services. Well, I have a new vendor I can highly recommend. It's McMannis Duplication and Fulfillment.

I met the owner, Jeff McMannis, when I was out in Goessel, Kansas, meeting with T.J. Rohleder a couple of months ago. He does all the duplication for T.J.'s company and fulfillment and mailing services for a lot of big players in direct marketing.

They have been a piece of cake to work with and their quality of service and products are first class. Several fulfillment companies I've tried in the past have made the entire process very difficult . . . and many were hit or miss when it came to reliability. McMannis has been awesome. One of the best I've ever used for both direct mail fulfillment and product/order fulfillment. If you have a need for their services, check out:

www.McMannisInc.com

Tell them Doberman Dan sent ya and they'll treat you like a VIP. (Actually, they'll treat you like a VIP even if you *don't* say you're a subscriber of mine. That's the kind of company they are.) So there's another great option for you . . . *and* I've taken away all your excuses for not doing all the stuff we've been talking about in this book that could easily . . .

DOUBLE Your Business . . . in 59 Days or Less!

Back to the SBCSS. Where did we leave off? Oh, I remember. We were talking about the SBCSS auto-responder series. We left off with this:

A couple days later, auto-responder #3 goes out. (By the way, as we get closer to the launch date, the frequency of your messages will increase . . . even to three or four a day on the day of the launch.) Tease, tease, tease. "Teach" them about your amazing new breakthrough product without revealing any "meat." Dan Kennedy is a master at this. Frank Kern is the online master . . . and he learned it from Dan Kennedy.

In other words, we still haven't started lifting our skirt. They can still only see our ankles . . . but they're *imagining* what's north of that. (And in many cases, our prospect's imagination is *much* better than the reality.) We're still just in the flirting stage . . . batting our eyes and playing coy. The only thing we want them to do is go to our page on launch day.

Ya dig? We're playing a game of seduction leading up to our highly anticipated event . . . our launch day.

What's that? You say you want to actually see how I would write a "teasing" email or blog post as part of this series? Geez . . . I guess I have to do *everything* for you, huh? OK . . . I'll do it . . . on one condition: You **take action** on what I'm teaching and actually implement your own SBCSS.

Deal? Okey dokey. Remember . . . the theme/hook of our launch is . . .

How to Get a Hard Body . . . without All the Hard Work!

Which was 100% swiped from T.J. Rohleder. (I'm not a plagiarist. He's a subscriber and said it was OK to swipe it.)

Let's say this is the third or fourth email of our series. The first few were fairly "blind"—we were only batting our eyelashes and showing ankle. Now we're starting to slowly and coyly "lift our skirt" a bit.

Subject line: **Contrarian secret for RAPID fat loss (HIGHLY controversial)**

Ya know what one of the biggest obstacles is to the success of your launch?

Getting Your Emails Opened!

Building a sub-list is a big help in overcoming that obstacle. Writing subject lines that arouse curiosity helps quite a bit too. That's what I'm trying to do here.

Onward.

Body Copy

Hi <Firstname>,

Confused about the BEST way to lose body fat?

You're not alone.

There's so much conflicting information from various "experts"... quite frankly, it's overwhelming.

But today I'm going to reveal a secret almost ALL of the "experts" don't know that can GREATLY accelerate your fat loss progress.

Many would consider it fat loss HERESY.

It's probably the exact OPPOSITE of what you've been told to do to lose body fat.

The good news?

It's brain-dead simple to do and you're going to LOVE it.

Even BETTER news?

You get to eat all kinds of DELICIOUS foods you were probably told were taboo.

Ready for the secret?

To lose body fat you need to ...

EAT MORE FAT!

That's right. Steaks, butter, eggs, heavy whipping cream in your coffee ... all the stuff you've been told will make you GAIN body fat will actually help you LOSE body fat.

BUT ...

... ONLY if you eat those foods in the correct combinations ... and at the exact times I reveal in my soon-to-be-released "Hard Body Without The Hard Work" fat loss system.

You can get all my best rapid and easy fat loss secrets this Tuesday, January 2 at 12:00 PM Eastern time at ...

www.HardBodyWithoutTheHardWork.com

See ya then!

Sincerely,

<Your name>

P.S. Tomorrow I'm going to tell you about the secret exercise I've discovered that helps you burn off body fat 377% faster than ANY other exercise you could possibly do.

And even better ...

It only take 2 minutes and 33 seconds to do ... and it's actually FUN!

Most people make a game out of it and look forward to doing it every day.

Keep an eye out for my message tomorrow.

~~~

Let's talk about this email for a sec and why I wrote what I wrote.

It *appears* I'm teaching and giving helpful information ... but what I'm *really* doing is telling them **what** to do without telling them how to do it. The "how" is revealed in the product ... which they have to pay for. They can't just eat fatty foods and get ripped. They have to know exactly what to eat ... in which combinations ... and at what times to eat each different combination ... none of which I disclosed in the email.

I reminded them of the launch date, launch time, and website, which, if you remember from the last chapter, has a countdown timer. You should remind them of these three things in every email you send.

VERY important: Look at the P.S. again.

That's what I call the "cliffhanger ending." Just like the old cowboy series. Our hero is riding to his imminent death off the end of a cliff while being pursued by bad guys in black hats. The episode ends at that point with the announcer saying, *"Will Cowboy Bob fall off the cliff to a grisly death? Is there any hope to save him from the pursuing heavily armed band of Black Bart's henchmen? Tune in next week for the exciting conclusion."*

Or something like that.

I'm building anticipation for the next email by teasing with something that is highly desirable or enticing to this particular niche. Now they'll be on the lookout for my next email and that should help with that open rate problem we always struggle with in email marketing.

You should use this "cliffhanger ending" technique in every message during your launch. Heck, you should probably use it in *every* email, period ... launch or not ... and whether you're selling anything or not. It works like crazy for building anticipation for your next message ... and getting higher open rates.

Every day during our launch your prospect is going to receive an email like that. On the day of the actual launch you'll send out an email like this in the morning:

Subject: Almost time

Body Copy

Hey <Firstname>,

The past two weeks I've been telling you all about how you can lose body fat as quickly as possible . . . and as easily as possible with my new "Hard Body Without The Hard Work" fat loss system.

Well guess what . . .

TODAY IS THE DAY!

At 12:00 PM noon Eastern time today, I'm finally making my ground-breaking "Hard Body Without The Hard Work" fat loss system available to a few lucky people like you.

But I only received 96 sets of the "Hard Body Without The Hard Work" fat loss system from the duplicating company.

And to be totally transparent with you . . . because of cash flow issues in my business . . . those are the ONLY copies I will have for a while.

Once they're gone, they're gone.

And it might be another eight to ten weeks until I'm able to order any more copies from the duplicator.

So if you don't want to miss out on getting the fastest, most effective and EASIEST fat loss secrets available today . . . get yourself to . . .

www.HardBodyWithoutTheHardWork.com

. . . at EXACTLY 12:00 PM noon Eastern time today.

There are 5,656 people on this special early notification list and I just KNOW all 96 copies will be snapped up quickly.

So don't miss out on the most effective secrets EVER to getting the body you've always dreamed of . . . without the hard work.

At 12:00 PM noon Eastern time today, go here:

www.HardBodyWithoutTheHardWork.com

My brand new "Hard Body Without The Hard Work" fat loss system will be available then.

See ya at noon!

\<Your name\>

P.S. I'm not joking . . .

I really only have 96 copies available.

There is so much stuff included with the "Hard Body Without The Hard Work" fat loss system, it was fairly expensive to get everything duplicated.

I just didn't have the cashflow right now to order more than 96 copies.

If you miss out on one of these original 96 copies you're gonna kick yourself. Because it might be another two months (or longer) until I'm able to order more copies of the "Hard Body Without The Hard Work" fat loss system.

So don't drag your feet and miss out.

At EXACTLY 12:00 PM noon Eastern time TODAY go here:

www.HardBodyWithoutTheHardWork.com

~~~

I hope it goes without saying you need to find your own reason for fast action . . . and it better be a good one. The cashflow situation I wrote about above is a common problem for small businesses and, even though it's just an example, it's a believable reason for the limited supply . . . thus encouraging fast action on your prospect's part.

Or . . . you can use the same countdown timer we talked about in the last chapter and, once your product launches, reset the countdown time to only 24 or 48 hours. After that, your prospects can no longer buy the product at the introductory deeply discounted price and the price goes up by 50%. Or another option . . . they miss out on some very enticing bonuses . . . or a combination of both higher price *and* missed-out-on bonuses. Anything to get all the "fence sitters" (and there are a *lot* of them) to take prompt action or they'll lose out on something valuable.

The day of your launch, take the above message and . . .

Wash, Rinse, Repeat!

In other words, use that as a swipe, change it up a bit, and send out several emails throughout the day reminding them of the countdown or updating them on how few sets are left at the special introductory discounted price. Keep sending out reminder emails until the very last few minutes of the deadline. Three, four, five, or more messages are required if you don't want to leave any money on the table.

Will you get a lot of opt-outs with this frequency? Maybe. Maybe not. But who gives a flying fart? Do you really want to keep paying to have people on your list who are only mooches and don't want to buy your stuff? Let the mooches opt-out. They're doing you a HUGE favor. Being a successful marketer not only requires you to *attract* qualified prospects to you . . . it also requires you to *repel* certain people.

Since this is a sub-list made up of people from your main list who are highly interested in this topic, your opt-out rate should be fairly low. Again, don't worry about opt-outs. It's a dumb metric to track anyway. Go back to Direct Marketing 101 and refresh your memory about the *most* important metric . . . the one you *should* worry about . . .

Return On Investment!

Oh yeah. One last thing I almost forgot. After you've announced the launch several times to your sub-list, you should give the people on your main list the opportunity to buy also. You can send two or three messages to skim the cream off the top that didn't opt into your sub-list . . . or maybe came in after you sent out the messages announcing the sub-list.

We're just trying to flush out as many buyers as possible, as many ways as possible.

Before I show you how to put this bad boy on auto-pilot so you have an evergreen marketing system instead of a one-shot thing, let me reveal one of my little secrets that could very likely . . .

Double or Triple Your Launch Sales!

Ideally, about seven days prior to your launch date, we'd like for a series of direct mail pieces to start arriving in your prospect's mailbox . . . and arrive with as much "theater" as we can afford. If your product is a Lear jet you could probably afford to hire Brinks to deliver a locked Halliburton metal briefcase to your prospect's office . . . containing a video player with a personalized video message and personalized four-color materials. Oh yeah . . . instruct the Brinks guard to arrive with the briefcase handcuffed to his wrist and advise the prospect that for security reasons, the code to open the briefcase will arrive later that morning via FedEx. Can you imagine the stir that would create at the office? And the curiosity you'll arouse while that guy is waiting for FedEx to arrive with his briefcase code?

Now *that* is theater.

Obviously you can't afford to do that if you're selling $497 DVD sets . . . but you *can* do some cool affordable stuff that accomplishes the same thing. And how, pray tell, do I expect you to do that? Oh, come one! You should know how my demented mind works by now. The answer is simple: We're going to use direct mail delivered with an inexpensive form of theater known as . . .

Grabbers!

For only a few cents per prospect we can get a similar (but admittedly lesser) reaction as the guy who got the briefcase delivered by Brinks. For examples, check out:

www.3dMailResults.com

So . . . your prospect will ideally receive a series of at least three direct mail pieces delivered with theater starting approximately seven days before the launch. The purpose? Same as the email series . . . build curiosity and anticipation for the launch.

Say what? You want *another* example? Geez! I have a better idea: How about you cut me a check for $40,000 plus 5% royalties on gross revenues and I create the whole launch process for you? Not in your budget? Not a problem. Instead of writing an example of a launch promotion direct mail piece, how about I give you an example of a direct mail *opener* and let you do the rest. You'll learn a lot more that way than having me do everything for you. (Unless you *do* want to write me that $40,000 check.)

Anyhoo . . . how about this for starters: Attach a $1 million dollar bill from 3DMailResults.com to the top of your letter . . .

. . . and open like this:

Dear <Firstname>, [You *do* know personalization is an easy and inexpensive way to bump up your response in direct mail, don't you?]

As you can see, I've attached a $1-million dollar bill to the top of this letter.

Why have I done this?

Two reasons, actually:

1. What I have to share with you is so important I needed a unique way of getting your attention. And with all the junk mail we get, I wanted to make absolutely *sure* my message stood out from the crowd. *And...*

2. Since what you're about to discover is a secret unknown by 98.7% of doctors, nutrition experts, and fitness trainers that can practically *force* fat off your body as quickly as possible... **making you LOOK and FEEL "like a million bucks"**... I thought the $1-million dollar bill was an appropriate attention getter.

Here's what it's about:

[Yadda yadda yadda.]

Don't forget...

This coming Tuesday, January 2, at 12:00 PM Eastern time you can get all my very best rapid and easy fat loss secrets here:

www.HardBodyWithoutTheHardWork.com

[Yadda yadda yadda.]

Sincerely,

<Your name>

P.S. [Yadda yadda yadda]

~~~

Yeah, it's what seasoned direct marketers know as the "tired old dollar bill letter." Got news for you, Bubba. It might be old but it sure ain't tired. It's still working like crazy... *especially* in markets outside the "make money" niche that almost *never* receive unique and creative direct mail pieces like this. (Heck, I'm using it in the "make money" niche and it's working better than ever.) In addition to the emails your prospects are receiving, imagine the impact of getting a series of three letters sent in lumpy envelopes with attention-getting grabbers announcing your launch. If your prospects have even the teeniest, tiniest, little bit of interest in your product, your launch is going to be hard to ignore.

Most online marketers I know are fairly lazy so they probably won't invest the little bit of time and money required to do this stuff. Their loss. That's why smart guys (like *moi* . . . and very soon *vous*) can pull out a lot more money from promotions like this . . . with only a little bit more effort.

Bear with me for a few because I gotta back up for a sec. Everything I revealed in the last chapter and everything in this chapter has been leading up to the launch of your new product . . . which entails sending them to your sales page at launch time. But what if you don't want to spend weeks or months writing copy for your launch website . . . and don't have the money to hire somebody like me to write it for you . . . which will also take weeks or months?

Wouldn't it be nice to implement your SBCSS without investing the weeks and months required to create a sales page? How about instead of building excitement and sending them to a sales page, we build excitement and anticipation for . . .

An Online EVENT!

That event can be a teleseminar or webinar. Yes, you still need to write copy in the form of a script or outline . . . but it doesn't have to be a word-for-word deal like a sales letter.

Is it *better* than a sales letter? At this point, I'm not sure. It *might* convert better than a sales letter. There's only one way to find out . . . and we'll explore that later when we turn all this into an evergreen marketing funnel on auto-pilot.

You're getting the idea here, right? This ain't exactly rocket surgery.

Basically we're . . .

- Building excitement and anticipation for our launch date . . .
- Using the power of the law of reciprocity.

We've given away some cool info, videos, audios, special reports, etc., during this process. We've provided some good value to our prospects and now they feel indebted to us. (That's the law of reciprocity in action.) After all, when somebody does you a favor or gives you something, most humans feel a strong and almost immediate need to reciprocate. Based on almost two decades of direct marketing experience . . . and an almost lifelong study of human nature . . . many actually *will* reciprocate by . . .

Buying Your Product!

Exactly the reaction we want! (I love it when a plan comes together.)

Look, I'm not going to dot every "i" and cross every "t" for you. I've given you *plenty* to work with from these last few chapters. It's now up to you to do a little work and fill in the blanks, OK? Because . . . I want to move on to the part where this all gets *really* exciting:

Putting The Whole Kit and Kaboodle on Auto-Pilot . . .

Now you don't just have a "one-shot and gone" sales boost for a few days . . . you have a **sustainable new *asset* in your business that gets better and better with time.** How? Well, you can't tweak and improve your launch when you're in the middle of it, can you? But you sure as h-e-double-hockey-sticks can tweak and improve it *afterward*. That's one of the many advantages of reusing all the content from your launch and putting the whole system on auto-pilot. And here's how we're going to do that.

- **Your launch emails.** This one's a piece of cake. Simply copy the broadcast messages from your launch and paste them into an auto-responder in the proper sequence. That's it . . . you're done with this for now.

- **Repurpose the squeeze page you used to get people from your main list to your launch sub-list.** Put it on an evergreen URL you can drive traffic to on an ongoing basis.
- If you used an event like a teleseminar or webinar for your launch, set up an evergreen replay on a service like www.stealthseminar.com/, developed by one of my subscribers, Geoff Ronning.
- Contact all your affiliates (especially the ones who didn't promote the launch) and give them the materials they need to add this evergreen promotion to their auto-responder series. Now that everybody and their brother isn't promoting this all at the same time, they might be a lot more open to promoting for you.

This is when things start to get exciting. Instead of a one-shot deal, you now have an ongoing funnel that can be evaluated, measured, and continually tweaked for better and better performance. How? That's easy . . .

- Split test different email subject lines . . .
- Test different offers . . .
- Test different price points . . .
- Offer a three-pay or "30 day hold" option . . .
- Test a video sales letter against a sales page . . .
- Ad infinitum . . .

Because you now have an ongoing stream of prospects opting into this particular funnel, you can constantly test different variations on your control (the messages and copy you used for the original launch) trying to beat its performance.

What If You Have a Brick and Mortar Business?

A smart brick and mortar business owner collects contact info from prospects and customers just like direct response and online business owners. So, I'm assuming if you own a brick and mortar business you already have email and snail mail addresses for *all* of your customers . . . and a good percentage of your prospects. If you have that, you can easily adapt this SBCSS process for your business too.

You have several unique advantages over direct response/online business owners. You can build toward an actual in-person/in-store event . . . which can create a lot more theater than an online event. Depending on your market (and budget, of course) this event can be quite the shindig . . . and could wind up being the talk of the town.

One more unique advantage you have over the direct response and online business owners is . . . you can tell your customers and prospects to invite their friends and family to come with them. Heck, you could even incentivize them with high-value gifts and prizes based on how many people they bring. It's a proven referral technique that could not only bump up sales from your launch . . . it could quickly and easily . . .

Double or TRIPLE
Your Customer and Prospect Lists!

In addition to the email and direct mail promotions, you could add a phone call to the sequence, personally inviting your prospects and customers to your in-store event. You might be surprised at how many more people that one little addition can bring to your event. It's just one more big advantage you have as a brick and mortar business.

Anyhoo . . . it's a lot easier to take action, be positive, and enjoy life when the sun is shining and the birds are singing (like in the Disney movies), when everything's going your way, and your business is raking in the bucks by the wheelbarrow full.

But what do you do when everything is *not* going your way? You're stuck in a torrential downpour without an umbrella, you're trapped in a mind-numbing j-o-b you despise, the "lifestyle business" you're trying to get off the ground is hemorrhaging money like a stuck pig, the bill collectors are hounding you day and night . . . and "the wolf is at the door."

Never fear, my dear faithful reader. During the more than 20 years of my direct marketing career I've been in that position numerous times. It's all part of the entrepreneurial experience.

I've seen so much money come in, so quickly, it literally scared me. I've also seen it go out 10 times faster than it was coming in.

I've been legally bankrupt once and technically bankrupt at least four other times.

I've been homeless and lived in my car with Donner the Doberman for a period of time when "movin' on up" meant I'd made enough money to feed Donner and enjoy a can of sardines myself . . . with enough money left over to stay in a fleabag motel. And forced to sleep with one eye open and a gun under my pillow because my next door neighbors were prostitutes and crack dealers. I am *not* making this up.

Am I proud of that?

Hell, no.

In fact, I felt like such a worthless loser I might have been tempted to lick one of those South American frogs and fritter away a day or two in la-la land, avoiding reality. That is, if I had access to a South American frog at the time. (Do they sell those on the black market or something?)

I've also had to deal with a soul-depleting, mind-numbing j-o-b I hated, multiple businesses going under, mounting debts, and more . . . all while discovering my starter wife was having an affair and my mother was in a coma dying of cancer.

Life can really suck sometimes, can't it?

It can pin you to the mat and ruthlessly pummel you to a bloody pulp if you let it.

Or, hey . . . maybe it's just me.

Maybe I'm the only one who has to deal with this kind of stuff while also dealing with health problems (both my own and close family members) that could quickly turn fatal.

Maybe you've been blessed with a multimillion dollar trust fund from your family, you have perfect health, everybody in your family is healthy, whatever you touch turns to gold, and life always goes your way.

I hope so . . . but I highly doubt it.

Life can get really tough. Even more so for us daring folks who choose to live by our wits instead of settling for a secure paycheck from some big fat corporation or a looting blood-sucking government entity.

So what's the secret to getting through when everything turns to dog doody?

What do you do when the wolf is at the door and you need to generate some money fast?

You might not like this but . . .

The Time to Dig Your Well Is BEFORE You're Thirsty!

All those years spent like a zombie in front of the glowing blue light in your living room could have been invested building an income stream you could rely on now when you really need it.

But let's not berate ourselves for what's in the past . . . let's get to doing something . . . *anything* . . . **right now in the present . . . the only time we really have.**

Here's my big secret: The one I always rely on it when I need to generate money fast . . .

There Are Gold and Diamonds Hidden in Your List!

You just have to grab some tools and start mining them.

By the way, that could be any list you have. Even your Christmas card list if you're *really* desperate. But I'm talking specifically about the list of people who have previously or are currently doing business with you …

Your Customers, Clients, and Patients!

Before I sold it, my "go to" list when I needed to generate money fast was always my bodybuilding supplement business list. Both email and snail mail … suspects, prospects, and buyers.

If you're a service provider, like a copywriter, graphic designer, or consultant, it could be your past and current client list. (When was the last time you touched base with your past clients and asked if they had any pending projects you could work on? It's way easier doing *that* than getting a new client.)

Same thing with the customer list for *any* kind of business … online or brick and mortar. After you get a new customer, how often do you ask them to buy something else? The answer to that question for just about every business I look at is …

Not Often Enough!

Want to ensure you get a great response to the offers you send to your customer list?

Sell them exactly what they most want to buy.

In many cases that will be more of the same of their original purchase. That's one of the reasons I like the supplement business so much. Even if you start with only one product you've got an automatic back end built in. You can sell them another bottle when they run out in 30 days or you can enroll them in a monthly auto-ship program.

How do you know what your customers most want to buy?

That's easy...

Ask Them!

There's no need to speculate or go to the trouble of creating or acquiring products your customers won't buy. All you have to do is create a little survey with SurveyMonkey.com and they'll tell you *exactly* what they want to buy. Then find the product/service they want or have it created... or find somebody else who has that product/service and do a joint venture with them.

Simple, right?

When you're in a tight spot you don't have weeks and weeks to work on your offer and obsess about every single word choice in your copy... you need to get an offer out *yesterday*. So sit down and crank out your offer ASAP.

Want an example?

One of my *Marketing Camelot* subscribers, (http://MarketingCamelot.com) Rachel Sonneson, sent me this letter just the other day and it's a perfect example of how to touch base with your customers.

> **Celebrate Josh's Homecoming With 18% Off Your Next Order**
>
> Why have I attached yellow and green ribbons to this letters ?
>
> I'm having a Homecoming Sale to celebrate my son, Josh, returning from Afghanisthan and the ribbons seemed appropriate.
>
> Here's the deal.
>
> Josh is part of the 82 Airbourne Division so you save 18% on all orders placed by 4 PM, August 24 . (100-82=18)
>
> Why August 24th ?
>
> That's when my inside source tells me his unit will be heading home but please don't tell.
>
> My Source that he/she was NOT Supposed to let anyone know. The US government doesn't want the exact date leaked to the media.
>
> So do me a favor and keep the date under your hat and don't call CNN.
>
> What to do next.....
>
> **To take advantage of the Homecoming Sale and save 18% call or email me with your order no later than 4 PM, Friday, August 24, 2012.**
>
> Talk soon,
>
> Rachel Sonneson

I love its simplicity and brevity. She gets right to the point, gives a good reason why she's making the special offer, and then gives her call to action. She included her phone and email as part of the call to action but I deleted that for privacy purposes.

Sure, this could be improved, but check out the results:

The letter was sent in a hand-addressed envelope to a micro list of only 20 past customers. Yellow and Army green ribbons were attached to the top as grabbers.

From this promotion she got three orders and one email acknowledging receipt of the letter. (My bet is that will soon turn into an order.) That's a 15% conversion rate from which she made a net profit of about $1,000.

I'm guessing her cost per piece was around .55/each or less. So a total investment of $11 to net $1,000.

That's a 9,000% Return on Investment!

I love it when somebody connects the dots and sees that the back end is where the *real* money is.

I don't know how much time Rachel invested in writing this letter but I bet it wasn't a lot. What's keeping you from doing something similar? You could bang out a letter like this during commercial breaks while watching the idiot box. God knows how much money you're giving up every month by *not* doing this.

I've said it before and I'll say it again:

Getting a new customer is like pushing a bicycle up a steep hill. (Since 2008 it's more like pushing a Harley Davidson up a steep hill.)

But making a sale to an *existing* customer is like coasting downhill on that bike.

Your list is where you go when you need money fast. It contains untold amounts of money you're probably leaving on the table every month. It only takes a little "mining" to acquire all that gold you've been stepping over.

That's all well and good, DD . . . but I need money right now and I don't have a list.

OK . . . let's tackle this problem together. You've heard of using OPM (other people's money), right? Well, if you don't have your own list I'm going to suggest you use OPL . . .

Other People's Lists!

Somebody, somewhere has a list that would be ideal for your offer. You just need to present a joint venture opportunity to them that could put some decent coin in their pocket.

Just for fun, let's say you've been one of those people cramming info into your cranium the past several years but never implementing anything. So you got nuttin'... no list and no product. You're completely starting from scratch.

Why not seek out a JV partner with an established biz and customer list in a niche you like? You could offer to survey his list, find *exactly* what his customers want to buy, do all the work, create the product, offer it to his list, and give him a portion of the profits. As a business owner myself I would find that offer quite appealing.

Sure, you're going to have to invest a little sweat equity putting this deal together... but isn't a chance to get access to a totally kick-booty list worth it? If you understand everything we've been talking about in this chapter, the answer to that is an unequivocal "YES!"

Look, I'm afraid if you haven't yet grasped the fact that you're leaving a small fortune on the table every month and seriously impeding your business's growth by not properly working your back end you're probably beyond all hope.

I want to move on to another topic now but before we do that I'm going to beat a dead horse just to be absolutely sure you get it:

You're Not Contacting Your Customers Often Enough!

~~~

Now go plant your booty in a comfy chair, grab your favorite beverage, and let your Uncle DD tell you a titillating tale. (My tale will be *much* more titillating if your choice of beverage is an adult libation.)

Ahem...

Once upon a time, there was a man named King Gillette. Gillette was known as an eccentric fellow ... but by all accounts, there was nothing really special about him.

Nobody expected much more from him than they expected from the millions of other human beings inhabiting the Earth at that time. They would be born, consume, produce a new generation of little do-nothing consumers, and die ... without ever improving this world by even one teeny-tiny iota. Most were expected to live their entire lives without leaving even the most *minuscule* mark on humanity. (Sadly, the exact same as we expect from most people today.)

But ... none of that prevented King Gillette from becoming a HUGE success ... albeit rather late in life.

A bit of back-story on our protagonist: Gillette was a traveling salesman for the Crown Cork and Seal Company, which marketed the first major disposable product in America ...

Bottle Caps!

Yeah, these handlebar mustache-wearing, old-timey dudes were making a frickin' fortune on mundane ole disposable bottle caps.

But I digress. (And I temporarily broke the Alistair Cooke-type character I was trying to emulate while waggishly weaving this whopper of an anecdote.)

[PREGNANT PAUSE]

Unlike the rest of his colleagues at Crown Cork and Seal, Gillette had a dream. (It all starts with a dream, doesn't it?) He wanted to be much more than just a traveling salesman. Day in and day out, he vividly visualized himself a victoriously wealthy man with his own business empire.

But unlike most people who dream of a better life, Gillette actually *did* something about it. He saw the success his employer was enjoying selling disposable bottle caps and he wondered how he could model their success in a business of his own. But he was clueless about exactly how to do that to build a successful business for himself and his posterity.

After racking his brain for weeks without success, Gillette decided to use his own version of my mentor Gary Halbert's famous "potato box" secret. Instead of rooting through a massive swipe file, he painstakingly pored over the dictionary, word by word, looking for an idea . . . *any* idea. A spark of inspiration for something he could invent, make, or publish . . . and sell over and over again to his customers . . . just like Crown Cork and Seal was doing with their disposable bottle caps.

Gillette had not gotten very far with his "potato box inspiration search" when an idea hit him on the chin . . . literally.

He was shaving one morning with one of those straight razors all the barbershops of the time used. The blade had become dull so he had to go out and get it sharpened. That's when his breakthrough came . . .

A New and Safer Way to Shave!

In his own words . . .

> *"I saw it all in a moment . . . the way the blade could be held in a holder. Then came the idea of sharpening the two opposite edges of a thin piece of steel, thus doubling its service, and then came the clamping plates for the blades, with a handle centered between the edges. I stood there in a trance of joy."*

Gillette went to work developing a safety razor with disposable blades. That way he would only have to get a customer once. Then he could continue to sell them replacement blades over and over . . . for years and years.

What he didn't anticipate were the challenges that followed. You see, ideas are a dime a dozen. A great idea and $50 will buy you a small cup of coffee at Starbucks. The REAL value is in the *implementation* of a great idea.

The implementation part is where Gillette ran into his first roadblock. He knew practically nothing about creating a mechanical product … and even less about working with steel. With materials and tools bought in a Boston hardware store he cobbled together a crude model.

Was Gillette heralded as a brilliant inventor and future business mogul who would establish an empire that would prosper for the next 118+ years?

Ummm … not quite.

He was criticized, ridiculed, and laughed at … even by the people you would most likely expect to support him … his "friends" and family. (If you've ever attempted to stick your head above the crowd this probably sounds familiar.)

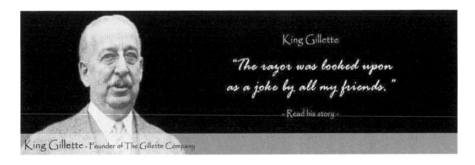

Who's Laughing Now?

From 1895 to 1900, Gillette couldn't get any technical advice from experienced craftsmen to improve his invention. Instead, they preferred to criticize and dismiss him as a weirdo. And … instead of financial assistance from the potential investors he approached, all he ever got was discouragement and criticism.

For five long years the only "help" Gillette had was his own persistence and unwavering faith. Five l-o-n-g years of continuous ridicule and rejection ... and I imagine what appeared to him as darn near zero progress.

But he persisted despite everything.

Then, as often happens when one has a single-minded stubborn determination to succeed no matter the obstacles, Gillette finally got a break. Two businessmen introduced him to William E. Nickerson, a graduate of the Massachusetts Institute of Technology. Nickerson saw the potential of this new-fangled safety razor and perfected the device for Gillette. A company was formed the next year and stock was issued to raise money.

Investors were skeptical at first, but a PWM (player with money) caught the vision and gave Gillette the seed capital he needed. Finally, after eight painfully long years of rejection and disappointment, in 1903 the company started production in a tiny, dingy, and dark room in Boston. American men soon began to respond to the safety, time-saving, and money-saving themes in Gillette's early ads.

An interesting little sidetrack: Have you ever noticed that many of the old-timey ads used direct response style copy?

Like this one:

Supplement Marketing Secrets

And this one:

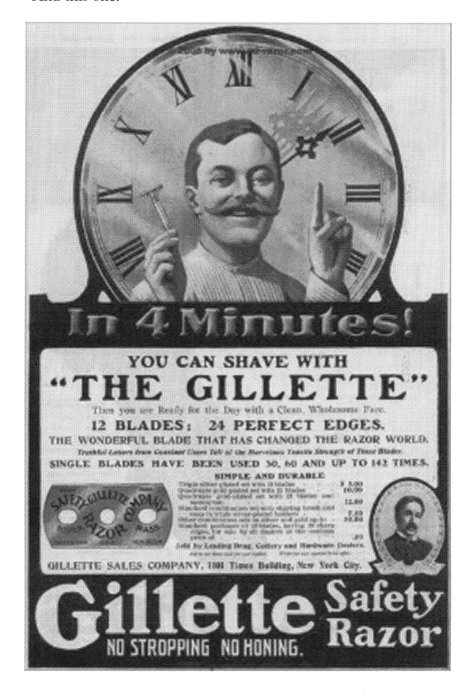

Back to our titillating tale: (I really like saying "titillating.")

In 1904, Gillette sales totaled 90,844 razors and 123,648 blades. The following year, four times as many razors were sold and ten times as many blades. By 1917 the company was selling more than 1 million razors a year and 120 million blades! Not bad for an eccentric guy with an idea laughed at by all the business "experts" of the day, huh?

A true entrepreneur, King C. Gillette was always looking for innovative marketing ideas to get his safety razor into the hands of more and more customers. The advent of World War II and the huge influx of new Army recruits turned out to be one of Gillette's biggest marketing breakthroughs. He came up with the idea of "gifting" one of his safety razors to every man entering the armed forces.

You see, Gillette knew he could take a loss on the razor because he would make it all back (and more) with the ongoing sales of the blades. His marketing team improved on this idea and instead of *giving* away the razors and taking a loss on the front end, they sold the government 4.8 million razors at cost and let Uncle Sam present them to the new military recruits.

Imagine the continuity income guaranteed to Gillette from acquiring . . .

5 Million New Customers . . .
Practically Overnight!

The best part? Gillette's blades were the only ones that fit his proprietary safety razor, guaranteeing years of ongoing income.

After the war, the millions of soldiers introduced to the new habit of self-shaving continued this practice after returning to civilian life, providing King Gillette with **tens of millions in continuity income.**

In the process of building his business empire, Gillette had become a master of marketing. While most businessmen only focused on one-shot sales (much like business people of today), Gillette was one of the few businessmen of his day who understood lifetime customer value ... and understood the "back end" was where the money is *really* made.

In fact, just before the patents on his safety razor were about to expire in 1921, Gillette thwarted a flood of imitations by lowering the minimum price of his razor from $5 to $1. You see, Gillette's experience proved it wasn't important to make a profit on the razors ... and he could even afford to "go negative." He knew almost all of his income came from the sale of the blades.

Today the Gillette Company manufactures 10 million razors a year. And God knows how many replacement blades it sell every year. The back end potential simply boggles the mind, doesn't it?

Have you picked up on the point I'm trying to drive home with my titillating tale? (I can't seem to stop saying that word.)

You don't make money *getting* a customer ...

You Make 90% (or in Many Cases 100%) of Your Profits Selling to an Existing Customer!

So if you focus most of your time and money on just getting new customers, you're stepping over dollars to pick up pennies ... and missing out on a literal *fortune*. Amazingly, every business I've been hired to work with hasn't been working their back end enough to make maximum income from their customer base. Not a single one!

And we'll talk about how to correct that problem in just a minute. But before we get into that (and it could make you *obscenely* wealthy), let's talk about another HUGE mistake I see most business owners making that's preventing them from getting rich:

Mistake #1

Believing Good Marketing Can Overcome Bad Math

A *fatal* mistake I see a lot of business owners making ... even people who should know better.

Can we talk like rational adults for a minute? The 1% (or less) who can think logically and ignore that annoying "bullshit fairy" who, since you were born, has been filling your cranium with lies like:

- Santa Claus, the Easter Bunny, and the Tooth Fairy are real living entities ...
- There really *is* such a thing as a free lunch ...
- You can think yourself rich ... while sitting on your ass in front of the idiot box drinking beer and eating pizza. (If only!)
- The world really *does* owe you a living ... *and* ...
- That charismatic and likable sociopath with perfect teeth, Armani suit, and teleprompter is going to make sure you get everything the world owes you.

Are you one of the precious few who have decided to pull back the curtain and face the truth, no matter how painful it might be? Even if it means turning your back on a lifetime of conditioning? Great! Then you're one of the infinitesimally tiny number of human beings intelligent enough to evaluate **FACTS** (not beliefs backed by zero evidence) and realize the following unequivocal truths:

- No matter how much you're in love with your product ...
- No matter how *good* a human being you think you are ...
- No matter how much favor you think you've gained with your supreme being of choice because of your faith or works ...

- No matter how much you think the world desperately "needs" what you have to offer ...

- And *especially* no matter how much of a rock-star marketer or copywriter you believe you are ...

2 + 2 Will Never ... Ever ... EVER ... Equal 5!

Amazing I have to explain this to adults, isn't it?

You'd probably be surprised at how *often* I have to explain it. You'd be even more surprised if you knew the famous people (well, famous in *our* little world) I've had to explain this to. Recently that includes a *literal* household name who, in the past, had built a $100 MILLION supplement business. For some reason, he seemed to believe his past success could overcome bad math in the new venture he's trying (unsuccessfully) to get off the ground.

What am I ranting about?

You Can't Build a Business Based on Bad Economics!

For a direct response business (online businesses are direct response businesses—duh!), you need a *minimum* 6-to-1 mark-up. In other words, your selling price should be at *least* six times your product fulfillment cost. For our purposes, "fulfillment cost" is your product manufacturing expense plus whatever other costs are involved in getting your product into the hands of your customer.

And 6 to 1 is the absolute **minimum**. *My* preferable minimum is 8 to 1. Ideally, if you want to grow your business as quickly as possible ... and as big as possible ... you should have a 10-to-1 mark-up ... or even more.

These aren't just random numbers I dreamed up in my demented cranium. There's a very important reason for all this. You see, anything less than 6 to 1 and you're going to have a tough row to hoe. In fact, you might not even have a *real* business. Instead, you'll have a revolving cash machine. What's a "revolving cash machine?" It's when you see the cash come in . . . and watch as it all (and possibly more) goes out just as fast (or faster) as it came in.

Want to siphon off a little bit for yourself? Good luck with *that*. You'll have to decide which expense you'll cut to generate a teeny-weeny slice of profit. While this allows you to take a few bucks out of your revolving cash machine for yourself, inevitably it contributes to a downward trend that lowers your incoming cash flow . . . which makes it even harder to keep this "ruse" of a business going.

Anything less than the minimum mark-ups we've been talking about is going to severely limit what you can afford to pay to acquire customers, therefore significantly suppressing business growth. Or . . . it will slowly and painfully kill your entire business over time.

An example? Alrighty. Let's say you sell your "thang" for $100 . . . whatever that thang might be. (For all the anal-retentive spelling gurus, I *meant* to spell it that way.) That means your fulfillment costs can't be a penny more than $16.67. Ideally, your fulfillment costs on a $100 product should be $10 or less. That's one of the many reasons I like info products. A 10x mark-up is chump change. And 100x, 1,000x . . . or even a 10,000x mark-up is quite common.

Ignore my advice at your own peril. Many a brilliant marketer with a huge marketing budget—and even multiple millions in venture capital—has gone bust arrogantly believing they could be the first person in the history of the world to overcome faulty arithmetic.

Mistake #2

Failing to Create "Rivers of Revenue" from Your Customer Base

This is the entire point of the Gillette tale (which I *hope* you found titillating) that I just shared. This is what you want to set up with some (or all) of your products and services ... endless "rivers of revenue" (ROR).

King Gillette created one of history's greatest marketing models because he set up endless rivers of revenue. Mobile phone companies use the same strategy. They sell you a cell phone at or below their cost ... and in some cases, they can afford to *give* it to you ... because they make money on every phone call. Many times for years and years. Believe you me, they know almost to the *day* how long they keep a customer on average. And based on that information, they know exactly how much they can afford to spend to ...

"Buy" a Customer!

That's really all you're doing with your advertising and marketing, isn't it? The better your mark-ups, and the better you know your back end numbers, the more customers you can afford to buy. And the guy or gal who can afford to buy a lot of customers—as quickly as possible—is the person who will dominate that market or niche. Everybody else is left to fend for the scraps.

Speaking of great back ends ... (no, not Kim Kardashian, you pervert) ... how about the Apple iPod? Sure, it's a great piece of technology ... but its *real* raison d'être is to sell you songs for 99 cents through the iTunes music store. *That* is how they really make money ... and they've already sold more than 15 **BILLION** songs at 99 cents a pop!

Another "King" of marketing, Bob King, formerly the rainmaker marketing guy at Phillips Publishing (a wildly successful newsletter publisher) used to tell all his hired gun copywriters . . .

"We're not in the newsletter business . . . we're in the renewal business!"

Very sharp guy, Bob King. He understood that when you build long-term relationships with your customers instead of "wham-bam, thank you, ma'am" one-night stands, you don't have to reinvent your marketing wheel every year. You can begin each year secure in the knowledge that a big portion of your income is already locked in for the year because the majority of your customers keep coming back to buy more.

Another big benefit of this river of revenue (ROR) strategy? Your cost of acquiring a customer gets amortized over many years' worth of purchases, driving your average cost per sale way, way down.

My beat-a-dead-horse point is this:

Don't think in terms of just one-shot opportunities to make money. A one-shot sale or just one successful front end promotion is *not* a business . . . it's a money-making opportunity. And there's a *BIG* difference between business builders and opportunity seekers. Business builders make money long term. Opportunity seekers are always running in circles . . . jumping from one fad to the next. (Remember all the poor suckers who jumped on the Google AdSense bandwagon?)

A better way to think is this: How can I leverage a one-time transaction into a permanent and self-renewing river of revenue (ROR) from each and every customer? This kind of thinking will make an **enormous** difference in the wealth you acquire over the life of your business. *And* . . . it just might establish . . .

An Uber-Successful Empire
That Lasts Your Entire Lifetime,
Your Childrens' Lifetimes . . . and . . .
Your Childrens' Childrens' Lifetimes!

Just like King Gillette.

Alrighty, I've talked about *why* you should create RORs . . . now let's talk about *how*.

Back in January 2012, one of my Gold Mastermind Mentoring members started a biz on his kitchen table with nothing but his brain and a laptop . . . and his wife's *superior* brain.

He's now getting 500 or so new customers a day at an average price point of $65. He has ZERO fulfillment costs if a customer chooses the digital delivery option. If they choose the hard-copy version he only has a few bucks fulfillment costs. Multiply 500 new customers a day by 30 days . . . bringing in $65 each on the front end . . . and . . . well . . . *you* do the math. It might have *started* as a kitchen table business but it ain't no small potaters now.

With my help we've started to work on improving his back end income. With a front end like *that*, he's going to make *CRAZY* cash once we start maximizing his back end. One of the options we've been exploring is developing one of these RORs I've been rambling on about. Let's explore a worst-case scenario and see how that might affect his bottom line.

500 new customers per day x 30 days per month =

15,000 New Customers a Month!

Now let's say the conversion into his continuity program is absolutely horrid. We only get 2% of those new customers each month to sign up for continuity.

15,000 x 2% = 300 customers per month in continuity

Actually, with the strategy I have in mind, I expect we'll convert anywhere from 25% to 30%. He'd probably get more than 2% conversion into continuity even if all he did was put a one-line upsell on his checkout page. But we're playing with a worst-case scenario in this example, so we'll keep the conversion percentage ridiculously low.

Let's assume an average $30/month price point. I actually think we can get closer to $49 . . . but we're being conservative in this example, remember?

300 customers per month in continuity x $30 = $9,000 "river of revenue" business added each month.

Don't be a marketing Pollyanna like I used to be and assume most of your customers will stay in your continuity program for years and years. Some will. Others will stay on for several months . . . and others will leave almost as fast as they came in.

So in this example, let's figure on an average "stick rate" of three months. (Actually, with my stick program in place, I expect his retention will average at the very *least* five months.)

Let's play with these numbers and see what the next year could look like when this bad boy starts to build exponentially:

Check this out:

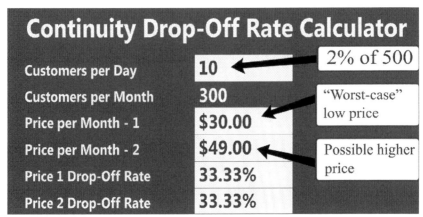

Supplement Marketing Secrets

This spreadsheet allows us to see the difference in potential income with two different price points, $30 and $49 in this example. I'm showing a 33.33% drop off each month to arrive at our average retention of three months.

Check this out:

PRICE1	Month1	Month2	Month3	Month4
New Customers	300	300	300	300
Total Customers	300	500	633	722
Monthly Revenue	$9,000.00	$15,000.30	$19,000.70	$21,667.77

This shows the cumulative total of customers in continuity and additional income for the first four months. Keep in mind, if my client bumps up his front end acquisition numbers, he'll have a bump in continuity customers, too . . . even at this crappy 2% conversion.

Total Yearly Revenue	PRICE1
45,000	NEW CUSTOMERS
11,164	YEAR END CUSTOMERS
$3,380,443.15	YEAR END REVENUES
112,681	TOTAL BILLING CYCLES
3	AVG BILLING

An extra $270k with a horrible conversion to continuity and a so-so stick rate. Worth doing to put an extra quarter million in your pocket? I'd say so.

Here's the first four months at the $49 price:

PRICE2	Month1	Month2	Month3	Month4
New Customers	300	300	300	300
Total Customers	300	500	633	722
Monthly Customers	$14,700.00	$14,700.00	$31,034.48	$35,390.69

And total yearly revenue at $49:

	PRICE2
45,000	NEW CUSTOMERS
11,164	YEAR END CUSTOMERS
$5,521,390.47	YEAR END REVENUES
112,681	TOTAL BILLING CYCLES
3	AVG BILLING

Things are starting to heat up a bit, aren't they? Now let's leave the price points and stick rate the same but bump up the conversion to the low end of what I think we can *really* get ... 25%:

PRICE1	Month1	Month2	Month3	Month4
New Customers	3750	3750	3750	3750
Total Customers	3750	6250	7917	9028
Monthly Revenue	$112,500.00	$187,503.75	$237,508.75	$270,847.08

Let's look at the end of year one with a 25% conversion:

Total Yearly Revenue	PRICE1
45,000	NEW CUSTOMERS
11,164	YEAR END CUSTOMERS
$3,380,443.15	YEAR END REVENUES
112,681	TOTAL BILLING CYCLES
3	AVG BILLING

	PRICE2
45,000	NEW CUSTOMERS
11,164	YEAR END CUSTOMERS
$5,521,390.47	YEAR END REVENUES
112,681	TOTAL BILLING CYCLES
3	AVG BILLING

Now let's keep everything the same as the previous example but bump the stick rate one additional month:

Supplement Marketing Secrets

With 4-month average stick rate

Total Yearly Revenue	PRICE1
45,000	NEW CUSTOMERS
14,525	YEAR END CUSTOMERS
$4,092,763.08	YEAR END REVENUES
136,425	TOTAL BILLING CYCLES
3	AVG BILLING

BIG difference!

4-month average stick rate

	PRICE2
45,000	NEW CUSTOMERS
14,525	YEAR END CUSTOMERS
$6,684,846.36	YEAR END REVENUES
136,425	TOTAL BILLING CYCLES
3	AVG BILLING

Looky here!

If you'd make an extra seven figures when your continuity customers stick one additional month, what would you do? Would you send a couple direct mail pieces and maybe have somebody give 'em a quick phone call? Maybe bribe them with a free gift? You'd be stupid not to, wouldn't-cha?

What are we going to sell these folks every month? That's the easy part. Here's a short list: monthly newsletter, CD, DVD, software, teleseminar, webinar, consulting, done-for-you marketing package, membership site, nutritional supplement ... heck, *anything* that eventually goes down the drain or toilet.

After more than 20 years in direct marketing I've never seen it more difficult or more expensive to acquire a new customer. It's CRUCIAL you use ALL possible methods to maximize your back end ... or soon, you might not even *be* in business.

In the next chapter I'm going to give you some more "maximum money" secrets. I'm also going to reveal customer service and merchant account challenges you'll probably deal with when selling on continuity.

Ignore these and you're toast. I'll also reveal a secret copywriters and consultants can use to create RORs by "annuitizing" their work.

One more for the road: *Titillating*. ☺

CHAPTER 6

The most reliable way for the little guy to get rich isn't the stock market or the lottery. It's developing a business with a customer base that keeps coming back to you over and over again.

The quickest way to go broke? Build a "revolving door" business where your customers go out just as fast as they come in.

Acquiring a customer and building a business these days is about as difficult and expensive as I've ever seen it. I truly believe those who don't get this concept . . . and continue to invest most of their time and marketing budget always chasing new customers . . . well, they probably won't last very long in this current economic climate.

But not you. Why? Because you've got *me* in your corner.

So let's *platicar* (that's Spanish for talk) about how you can help your customers stick around a lot longer . . . and spend more money with you, more frequently.

One important tip for doing that is simply adapt Robert Collier's admonition to copywriters. (If you haven't read *The Robert Collier Letter Book* you need to put that on your to-do list immediately.) Remember his oft-quoted advice? It was originally intended as a technique to write better copy. But you can also use it to keep customers for life, make maximum money from your customer base, and build a rock-solid business that endures for decades . . .

"Enter the conversation already taking place in your customer's mind!"

Here's what I mean. If you truly want to enter the conversation in your customer's cranium, you have to look at things from *his* point of view.

Why in the world should he continue to do business with you? What reason have you given him to be loyal to you?

An email every week or so? Get real. *Everybody* does that. (So much so that it probably just annoys him.)

Low price? You can bet your sweet booty that isn't gonna keep him loyal. Amazon or Walmart will kick your butt in that department. Or the hungry (and stupid) start-up will undercut you in a heartbeat. Scratch that one off your list too.

So what *will* keep your customer loyal to you?

REVERSE Customer Loyalty!

"*What's that?*" you ask befuddled.

I'm not talking about your customers being loyal to you . . . I'm talking about *you* being loyal to your customers.

Combine loyalty with REAL heartfelt appreciation and sincerely trying to see the world through their eyes and you've got one powerful combination.

Sadly, I almost never see this in *any* business. The prevailing attitude seems to be churn 'em and burn 'em. And believe me, Hoss . . . your customers can feel it.

And the problem is epidemic.

Think about it. Isn't every Internet marketing guru war story you've ever heard all about their "million-dollar day?" Some variation of "look how I make-money-in-my-underwear-by-only-pushing-the-send-button"?

They never talk about what they did for these new customers *after* the sale . . . or how long the customers stuck around, do they? Nope. The stories only focus on what a clever marketing genius the guru is. They never shine the spotlight on the *true* star of the show . . . the customer.

Hey, everybody likes a good success story. It's instructional to hear how a crafty copywriter or marketer discovered a unique hook that tripled sales. But nobody ever shares the most important part of the story. **How did the customer win?**

That brings us back to my "see the world through your customer's eyes" admonition. If you *really* want to do that, treat him like *you* would want to be treated. Simple, right? Well, since you're smart and have decided to use this powerful "reverse customer loyalty" secret . . . my question to you is . . .

What Happens after the Sale?

Sadly, with most businesses, not much.

Sure, entering them into an auto-responder series is better than nothing . . . but it sure ain't what it used to be. In fact, several of my clients this year have hired Ben Morris at Kristalytics.com to run his crystal ball-like semi-clairvoyant analysis on their customer lists. What we discovered was quite shocking. (To the clients, not me.) **And you can make a FORTUNE if you understand this important discovery.**

In every single analysis, we found the most affluent customers . . . the ones who make the biggest purchases . . . and most *frequent* purchases . . . are also the biggest email opter-outers. In fact . . .

At least 50% opt out immediately after getting the email receipt!

The remaining ones are usually long gone by follow-up message #1 or #2, at the latest. (I fall into this "immediate opter-outer" category, as do most other affluent people I know.)

At last, for the love of all things good and holy do you **FINALLY** understand why I keep brow beating you about incorporating offline methods to communicate with your customers? Geez, you can be thick-headed sometimes! I'm not just saying this stuff to listen to the sound of my own voice.

So knowing all this, my question again is, what happens after the sale? Or a better question, what *should* happen after the sale?

Well, what would *you* like to happen if you just made your first purchase with a company you had never done business with before?

Is getting a thank-you email something unique and unexpected? Would you feel the business owner went the extra mile to make you feel special? Not likely. It's expected . . . and everybody does it. It has darn near zero impact.

Would you feel kinda special if you got an email from the owner a couple days after the sale, sincerely expressing his gratitude? Maybe giving you some advice on how to use, profit from, or enjoy the product you recently purchased?

Yeah, that's kinda unique . . . actual customer follow-up to make sure you're happy with your purchase. I don't see a lot of that going on. We could count that as a somewhat positive "touch." It gets us some brownie points in our new "romance." Well, at least with the customers who haven't opted out, deleted the email unread . . . or never even received it due to a plethora of possible email delivery problems.

We're headed in the right direction . . . but it's *still* not enough. You put your heart and soul into creating the copy . . . you invested money you *could* have put into your pocket . . . and you probably haven't even made a dime yet. In fact, you've probably gone negative. So any reasonably intelligent person can see it only makes sense to foster this new relationship so the customer doesn't fly out the revolving door just as fast as he came in.

BIG SECRET #1 REVEALED

One of the most important phases in the customer romance . . . and a highly effective secret to building customer loyalty is what you do in the first 90 days of the relationship. I like to call this . . .

The Honeymoon Phase!

Ignore them during this phase and I can almost *guarantee* you'll always have a revolving door business.

So what are the most important and effective things we can do in our "reverse customer loyalty" program during the honeymoon phase? My experience has shown one of the most important "touches" is . . .

The Stick Letter!

And no, sending it via email won't work. It *must* be sent via good old-fashioned snail mail . . . or FedEx if your numbers warrant the extra expense. Whichever service you use, you need to send it in a creative way that makes it darn near impossible to ignore.

What else can we do during the honeymoon phase to make sure our customers stick around as long as possible?

How about . . .

- Quick order fulfillment . . .

- Quick resolution of problems or customer service issues...
- Quick and friendly no-hassle refunds...
- Unadvertised after-the-sale bonuses...
- Offer new and useful products and services in creative ways...
- Give away carefully timed ethical "bribes" and bonus gifts. (We'll talk more about this in a sec. It could be the breakthrough you need to *radically* increase your lifetime customer value.)
- Contact them more often with great content and relevant offers. (Everybody *greatly* underestimates how often they should contact their customers.)

In other words, design your customers' experience so they're treated the way you *yourself* would like to be treated.

Interestingly, as I was writing this chapter one of my trusted vendors, McMannis Duplication and Fulfillment, sent me a perfect example to show you.

This falls under the categories I mentioned a minute ago:

- *Unadvertised after-the-sale bonuses ... and ...*
- *Give away carefully timed ethical "bribes" and bonus gifts.*

Check this bad boy out...

Pretty cool, huh?

The gold hammer is to whack away on this massive (9"x12") chunk of chocolate to break it up into little pieces. I wanted to pick the whole damn thing up and gorge on this gastronomically gluttonous gratification but the Colombiana "forbade" it, bless her heart. She made me settle for much smaller pieces than I would have preferred. Me likey me some choc-o-late!

Anyhoo . . . how do you think McMannis's customers reacted to this big ass hunk of chocolate arriving completely unexpected? I already LOVE McMannis and wouldn't even *consider* taking my business elsewhere. After getting this unexpected gift, I'm an even MORE ardent supporter and promoter of McMannis Duplication and Fulfillment. And that could turn out quite profitable for them. When any of my clients or colleagues needs printing, mailing, duplication, or fulfillment services, who do you think I'm going to *fanatically* endorse?

Because their service and people completely R-O-C-K in the U-S-A, McMannis already had my loyalty. But stuff like this creates raving fans. Even ole DD learned an important "love your customer" lesson.

If you're not doing stuff like this, you oughta whip it out right this very second (a notepad, dummy) and figure out how to start treating your customers like gold. Like McMannis does. It's not just the right thing to do, it's an absolute necessity if you want to stay in business and prosper in our new economy.

I have an inside joke with friends and family members about a couple words I invented, *kringlebomber* or *kringler*, for short. (Never mind what they mean. Just know if I ever call you that, it's a term of endearment.) I found this bakery at ohdanishbakery.com that ships a pastry called a "kringle." I've sent and received them as gifts from friends who are hip to my little inside joke. My sister sent one that arrived just last night. (She's a "first class" kringlebomber.)

Now usually, they just send the kringle and a catalog. But this time I noticed a little extra surprise.

They included a full-color children's storybook. It elicited a *"cool!"* response from me and a *"Qué chévere!"* response from the Colombiana. I believe that's the exact response the kringle bakers were hoping for. Of course, it doesn't hurt that their origin story is woven into the book ... and their website is included on the back cover.

I bet people with children will keep this thing around a while. Heck, it might even be on several thousand bookshelves as we speak.

Kinda a cool little unexpected gift to endear the kringlebombers to their customers, isn't it? It probably only adds a buck or two to fulfillment costs but pays off BIG time on the back end.

One last example of unexpected little surprises for your customers:

I recently placed an order with 3dmailresults.com for some $1-million dollar bills I'm using as grabbers for a sales letter. About three days after the $1-million dollar bills were delivered, I got this in the mail:

Inside the card they included one of their $1-million dollar bills:

My mailing is only going out to a small but highly targeted list so I think I spent $200 or less with 3dmailresults.com. These guys have a big business so I'm certainly not a priority customer . . . yet the owner still took the time to send me a handwritten thank you.

That made a big impact on me . . . because after more than 20 years of being in business and spending millions of dollars with various vendors, I can count on one hand the number of companies that have expressed their gratitude with gestures like this.

Look, one of the most important and impactful "touches" you can make is a real honest-to-goodness handwritten card or letter. But if you're so slothful you can't be bothered with sending a REAL hand-signed card, here are a few options for a reasonable facsimile:

http://ink-a-note.com

http://www.bluebirdcards.com

https://www.sendoutcards.com

Any of these options are 100x's better than email . . . but *nothing* has the same effect as a card or letter really and truly signed in your own hand.

BIG SECRET #2 REVEALED

What are YOU including in your outgoing orders and sending to your customers after the sale to elicit a "wow!" response and encourage back end sales? You're leaving TONS of money on the table if you're not doing *something* like these examples.

And if you're not sending bounce-back offers in your outgoing packages, you're *really* missing the boat. After all, your customer is paying the mailing costs to send them a sales piece. You'd be a drooling mouth-breathing moron to not take advantage of that, wouldn't-cha?

Alrighty then. Would you like another big secret to keeping your customers with you as long as possible . . . *and* spending more money with you month after month?

BIG SECRET #3 REVEALED

Publish and mail . . .

A Monthly Newsletter!

Yes, it absolutely must be a good old-fashioned paper and ink newsletter sent via postal mail. *NOT* email, *NOT* a PDF delivered online, *NOT* a blog, *NOT* a membership site . . . *NONE* of that online stuff you want to do because you like to cut corners and pinch pennies.

Believe me, if those methods worked I'd be doing them . . . 'cuz it's the lazy way. But I've tested ALL the online delivery methods and not a single one even comes *close* to the ROI you'll get from a REAL honest-to-goodness. arrive-at-your-home-or-office, hold-it-in-your-grubby-little-hands newsletter.

What does a print newsletter do so well that nothing else can do?

It Builds a Friendship!

Customers, clients, and patients come and go, easily swayed by competitors offering even the teeniest tiniest of discounts. But friends . . . people you regularly break bread with and spend time sharing hopes and dreams ... they stick around *much* longer than just a customer. You don't leave your friends, do ya?

Think about this:

Every month my newsletter friends invite me into their homes as a welcome guest and we have a personal conversation. (TOO personal if they read my letter in the bathroom.) They know details about my life even members of my own family don't know.

For example, if you had read my newsletter, you would know the following intimate fine points about me.

- I cried on your shoulder after Donner the Doberman died.
- Your heart pounded when you pictured me (in your mind), 12-gauge shotgun at the ready, about to smoke a big burly drugged intruder in my bedroom, intent on harming my family.
- You know I suffer daily with chronic pain. And you know if the pain isn't keeping me from getting a decent night's sleep, the nightmares from the PTSD do a damn good job of it.
- You know I've made millions ... and lost millions.
- You know I've been so broke, I've actually had to live with my Doberman in a 10-year old piece o' crap Ford Taurus with no air conditioning.

The Colombiana is a very private person and she constantly busts my chops about revealing stuff she thinks should be kept private. But I share it for a reason. I'm trying to create a friendship ... and friends share intimate details of their lives.

I'd actually rather *not* share some of this stuff. Much of it is quite embarrassing to me ... but experience has shown that sharing this stuff helps people. And very recently, one of the more embarrassing things I didn't really want to reveal helped save a life ... literally.

People don't really buy products and services ... they buy YOU. And a newsletter (if it's done right) is an *intimate* form of communication from you. That's one of the biggest secrets of its success. The only thing more intimate is a handwritten letter, phone call, or in-person visit.

When subscribers (who I don't know from Adam) meet me in person, they treat me like an old friend they've known for years. *That* is the power of a print newsletter. I've not found anything that even comes *close* to replicating that effect.

Pete Lillo, aka Pete the Printer, sums it up quite succinctly . . .

"If you don't have a newsletter, you don't have a business!"

If you truly value your customers and want to keep them long term, you'll send them a monthly print newsletter. 'Nuff said.

We've been talking about *reverse* customer loyalty . . . you being loyal to your customers, not just expecting customer loyalty because they've bought something from you. That means you don't just forget about your customers and let them die on the vine if you haven't heard from them in a while. That's just plain dumb. You don't treat your friends like that, do you? (If you do, I doubt you have many friends.) You check in with them to make sure everything's OK, don't you?

So let me reveal one of my most important, most profitable and ridiculously crazy high ROI reverse customer loyalty secrets. (I should have listed this as #1 because it's the lowest hanging fruit/most profitable thing you can possibly do in *any* business.)

BIG SECRET #4 REVEALED

Keep in touch consistently and persistently with your inactive customers.

I have a client with a (now) rapidly growing business in the health market. During the past 60 days I helped take him from $400,000/month and quickly dwindling . . . to $620,000/month by the third week of January. We fully expect to pick up another $30k to $40k by the end of January. How did I do it?

Well, we did a LOT of things (that's another secret) but one of the *biggest* contributors to this rapid growth was simply going after the low-hanging fruit . . . the inactive customers. And we reactivated a LOT of them. We used "fusion marketing," a combination of multiple "touches," both online and offline . . . with each offline step timed very carefully to augment and support the online steps . . . and vicey versey.

It's a system I developed and perfected for my own businesses and without fail, it always pays off BIG time. Here's a template example of one of the initial letters I use in my "colossal cash crescendo" system:

> Dear <insert first name>,
>
> As you can see, I've attached a <whatever grabber you use> to the top of this letter.
>
> Why have I done this? Actually, there are two reasons:
>
> 1. What I have to share with you is vitally important for your health and happiness . . . and with all the junk we get in the mail nowadays, I needed a unique way to get your attention.
> 2. And . . . since what I have to share with you can <yadda yadda>, I thought the <grabber> was an appropriate eye-catcher.
>
> Here's what it's all about:
>
> Not very long ago you were a valued customer of mine. But for some reason I haven't heard from you. And that's been bothering me.
>
> I keep wondering . . . did I do something to offend you? Did I goof something up with your order?

The letter goes on to make two additional offers:

1. Some kind of no-strings-attached free gift they can get in the mail, email, or by digital download . . .

2. And a "we want you back" offer with a special preferred customer discount and lots of premiums and bonuses.

In the case of my client, he wanted to make it a little more difficult for me and reactivate inactive customers into a $100+/month continuity program. Kinda a big step to ask an inactive customer to take . . . but I was up to the challenge.

How did it go? Results are still coming in. And the final few steps in this multi-step system won't go out for another five to seven days . . . so I think we've only gotten 60% to 70% of all the results. But so far, without any sales from the remaining final steps, we've added an additional . . .

$60,000+ a Month in Continuity Income!

And this was money the client had been leaving on the table month after month for *years*. Although my retainer and royalty initially shocked him, after this campaign, he thinks my fees are a screaming bargain. If I can get him to agree to just one more step (my super-duper, secret, get-'em-off-the-fence step) we should add at *least* another $20,000 a month in continuity income before the fat lady sings.

I'd be willing to bet that YOU are sitting on a nice windfall like this too. Thar's gold in that there list of your'n. You just gotta go git it, pardner.

~~~

You've heard of the infamous "Google slap" haven't you? I think it was Perry Marshall who coined that phrase. Anyhoo, I've recently coined my own phrase for a lesser-known but just as insidious Google problem, robbing 10s of millions from thousands of entrepreneurs. I call it . . .

The Google Sucker Punch!

I've had a blog post draft about this in WordPress for some time now. Maybe one day I'll finish it . . . but it's so important, I want to reveal it to you first. And give you the tools and tactics you need to prevent it from stealing money away that *should* be yours.

So what's the Google sucker punch?

I'm glad you asked!

People Google *everything* ... and within six months many buy what they searched for. But most likely not from you. You're forgotten the very minute they click away from your website.

Maybe you've spent money on AdWords, CPV, banner ads, solo email, direct mail, space ads, or whatever online or offline advertising you do. Or ... if you're extremely lucky you've got organic search engine placement in the top 10 for certain buying keywords. (Enjoy it while it lasts. It'll be a short ride, I promise you.)

My point is, you got the searchers to Google you in one way or another. But only a small percentage are ready to buy right now. Google got them to come in the front door but most are immediately skedaddling out the back door.

That's the Google sucker punch ... and most online entrepreneurs are losing a lot of money because of it.

Unless you've done the work to capture the contact info, build a relationship, and stay in constant contact. *And* ... hopefully in that time you've turned them into, at the very least, a follower ... and preferably a ...

Raving Fan!

That's about the only way you can make almost darn sure they'll buy from you when they're ready instead of re-Googling (Ha! I just invented another word!) and buying from somebody else.

Speaking of followers and raving fans, let me give you some numbers I've been working on to help set your expectations about what kind of results you'll probably get. I've found a formula that seems to be a bit contrary to the typical 80/20 rule (Pareto Principle) . . .

1. 33% of people will dislike or hate you and your message . . .
2. 33% will be indifferent to you . . .
3. 33% will like you and what you stand for . . . if you actually stand for something . . . and . . .
4. Some of those "we like you" 33% will even become raving fans and supporters who continue to give you money quite frequently.

I realize that only adds up to 99% . . . and I have no idea about the remaining 1%. I believe they're incarcerated or in mental institutions (AKA my future retirement home) so that's why we don't count them.

At this point you might be asking, *"Dan, how exactly do I bond with my customers, build trust, and keep the 33% who like me sticking around long enough to turn them into buyers? And how do I turn some of those into raving fans?"*

Good questions. You're a lot smarter than you look. ☺

I realize this might sound rather self-aggrandizing but I think a good study of how to do that is . . .

This Book!

Look at the entire funnel to get someone into my *Marketing Camelot*. Most people probably found me through my blog at DobermanDan.com. Or my *Off The Chain* podcast on iTunes. Or one of my best selling books on Amazon.

With my blog and the emails that go out to blog subscribers, I try my best to attract the people who "resonate" with my message and what I stand for. If someone likes my blog, they're sure to like the *Marketing Camelot* even better. I try my best to bond with you through the blog by sharing stories, rants, successes, tragedies, and some intimate details of my life. *The Doberman Dan Letter* is more of me . . . except with the volume on 10. See, my volume knob is quite unique. It goes to 11. (That's louder than 10, inn't it?) Believe you, me ... there are very few people who could tolerate me with the volume on 11.

Anyhoo ... how I bond with people is simple. I let the DD personality shine like a beacon in everything I write. I can't control the percentages I just told you about. The only thing I can do is put myself out there in various media as often as I can. I only write for the people I know will "get" me ... and that is a *very* small percentage of the population.

Those who will hate me will hate me. (I actually enjoy writing things to repel those folks.)

Those who are indifferent ... well, if they stick around long enough I just *might* be able to convert a few ... but I wouldn't bet the farm on it.

Those who like me ... *those* are the people I attract and want to bond with. With the hope that a small percentage will turn into raving fans and stick around a long time.

So my formula is simple. I simply share my life with you and don't pull my punches. You get DD with all his scars and faults. In print (mostly), on webinars or videos, audios, and phone calls.

Could I write a different way or in a different "voice" to attract a different crowd? Sure. I do it all the time with various personal projects and work I do for clients.

My voice with you is mostly like I talk. But, if needed, I can write to a highbrow crowd. It's not the real me ... but I can do it. It's just like an actor playing a role.

Speaking of the "Marketing Camelot," let's talk about that for a sec. (http://MarketingCamelot.com)

Correct me if I'm wrong but I'm fairly sure I heard a voice in your head asking, *"Dan, why the 'Marketing Camelot' instead of saying newsletter subscription or membership? And why all this 'Knight of the Round Table' stuff instead of just calling us subscribers?"*

Another excellent question. (Man, you're sharp. I regret calling you a ninny earlier.)

So why do I do that?

Actually, a couple reasons:

1. It's the ideal I strive for and have had in my demented noggin since the beginning of this noble endeavor. I haven't achieved what I have envisioned yet. I'm still striving toward that goal . . . but I'm getting closer.

2. I want my connection to be more than just a newsletter. You see, I discovered (the hard way) that nobody really wants to buy a newsletter . . . nobody really wants to be a newsletter subscriber . . . and very few people even have an interest in learning anything new.

   But . . . a lot of people do have a deep-seated need to belong to something important . . . something bigger than themselves . . . a fraternity that stands for something . . . a group with a higher purpose whose goal is to make this world of ours a better place, some way . . . somehow.

   That is way more important than a newsletter. And many people will stick around a lot longer than the two-to-three month average retention most membership sites and continuity newsletters have (40% of my knights have been with me since day one of this noble endeavor).

Silly? Maybe to some. But I sincerely believe we can achieve this ideal.

Or come fairly darn close.

So, in my most humble (but always accurate) opinion, the takeaway is . . . if you want to attract and keep the 33% who like you and resonate with you and your message, you need to elevate whatever you're promoting to a higher ideal than just a membership, newsletter, blog, or eZine.

Ya dig?

You see, when I start a business, I'm in for the long haul, (however long I decide that will be) not the "make-a-quick-buck" mindset by burning through large numbers without a care. My goal is to establish enough trust to build a back end that endures for years.

Maybe decades.

If you listened to all the Internet marketing gurus during the past 10 years or so, they erroneously taught that online marketing was all about how many suspects were on your list. Or the number of followers you have ... or the number of Facebook likes you could get.

I guess all that chest-pounding and bragging about 250,000 suspects on a "cheap bastard" freebie give-away list sounds sexy and impressive ... until you've wasted years of your life and lots of cashola building the same ... and you realize what *really* matters to the bottom line is ...

Connection and Trust!

That is what fuels a business, not big numbers constantly running through a revolving door.

The key question is this:

Do your buyers feel enough of an affinity with you ... and trust you enough to keep coming back over and over, money in hand?

Rookies are constantly chasing big numbers, that in most cases are meaningless. Give me a list of 500 to 1,000 buyers who like and trust me (a small percentage of those will also be raving fans) and, in terms of net profit, I'll beat the pants off your 250,000 suspect list you built by giving away free stuff.

Trust doesn't just happen. You need a meticulously planned strategy that builds it over time.

Can you walk up to a stranger on the street, introduce yourself, and get them trust you after only a few minutes of chatting?

Highly unlikely. (Unless you're a very skilled con artist.)

It's the exact same thing with your clients, customers, and patients. They probably won't trust you the first time they meet you or stumble on your website. And telling them they can trust you ain't gonna make it happen either.

The only two things I've found to build trust are ...

1. Be trustworthy ... and ...
2. Build trust slowly over time.

In my more than 20 years in direct response marketing and serial entrepreneurship I've not found any trust-building shortcuts.

With all our high-tech tools and the latest and greatest technology, it still comes down to this:

Prospects Will Only Do Business with a Person They Trust!

Because that choice eliminates fear and makes your customer experience the warm and fuzzy feeling of safety.

You see, most people in this once formerly free republic live their lives in a constant state of fear. People are scared of just about *everything*. Many entities working in collusion have spent decades and trillions of dollars to create this mass fear ... but I digest. (I love it when people write me and say I misspelled "digress." Spelling gurus are born without a sense of humor I guess.)

With so many scaredy-cats living in constant fear, you'll stand head and shoulders above all the other choices in your market if you'll just do the simple things required to build trust.

And you need to start this trust-building process the very moment those suspects, prospects, and customers stumble into your little world. The longer you delay the process, the harder it is . . . and the more likely they'll go right back out your revolving door.

The time to do all this is *today*. Dig your well before you're thirsty, so when the time comes you can simply pump the handle and watch the water freely flow . . . as if you're tapped into an abundant spring.

You can't *make* trust happen . . . you create the conditions for trust to happen on its own. It's how you're rewarded for your investment of time, energy, and, most of all, caring. And *that* translates into long-term income.

Trust me. ☺

~~~

And now seems like the ideal time to transition into chit-chatting about exactly how to monetize all these customers. More specifically, how to . . .

Enjoy the MAXIMUM Possible Profits!

There are several ways to do that, ya know? Sadly, I see very few entrepreneurs who know how to do it. And they're leaving a *lot* of money on the table.

We don't need to get into any complicated math or any fancy-pants projections and spreadsheets. It's actually much simpler than that. The #1 most crucial thing you must do to ensure you enjoy the maximum possible profits from your business is . . .

Do Everything within Your Control
to Have Happy Customers!

Actually, there are two definitions of the word happy to be considered here. For you, happy means an overwhelming sense of joy and excitement as you see large deposits arriving in your bank account from the flood of sales you generate day after day.

For your customer, happy means merely satisfied ... or not *un*happy. That's really all most customers expect today. They're conditioned to accept that customer service sucks in this country. They're most certainly not accustomed to being thrilled by the companies they do business with.

But you *are* going to thrill them. Because the happier your customer is, the more repeat business you'll get. And when you get repeat business it's basically like being handed ...

Large Stacks of Cashola ...
for FREE!

Look, I'm going to share some stuff with you that might seem quite elementary.

I agree. It is elementary. But you ain't doin' it. So obviously you don't know it yet. So we're going back to kindergarten in order for this lesson to penetrate that mulish melon of yours.

'Cuz You're Leaving Potential
MILLIONS on the Table!

Let's take you back to Direct Response 101 for a minute. Let's say you sent out a letter or an email to a customer that said ...

> *Dear Customer,*
>
> *I'm kinda hard up for cash at the moment and I'd really like a new Ferrari and a 10,000-square foot, eight-bedroom house.*
>
> *I was wondering if you would be so kind as to send me $100.*
>
> *Thanks a bunch.*

Very truly yours,

Sir Richard of Cranium

If the customer were crazy enough to send you $100, you would have just completed a direct response transaction. Capiche? This is the basis of the whole direct response business. People receive your message and they send you money. Sounds good, right? There's just one little teeny-weeny factor we've left out of this equation. You usually have to send your customers something in return for their money. Ain't that a bitch? I mean, imagine how much more money you could make if your customers weren't so small-minded and selfish. How petty of them to actually want something in return for their money.

Whatever. It is what it is. So you gotta send them something. What you send them and how you send it can make the difference between having a thrilled customer who continues to spend money with you month after month . . . or an unhappy customer who will never spend another dime with you for as long as they live. In fact, there's a good chance they'll ask for a refund or do a chargeback.

Yessiree, bub. What you do *after* you make a sale is just as important, if not more important, than what you do to get a sale. (*Especially* if you get your customers on continuity.) Get this right and you'll have a crazy profitable business with extraordinarily high customer retention. Get it wrong and you'll see the money go out just as fast (or faster) than it came in.

Next chapter I'll reveal a marketing secret, complete with tested and proven swipes you can use immediately to rake in a ton of that "FREE money" you've been missing out on for so long.

I've seen some BIG results from this system. Like a 2x bump in NET . . . in only a few months. It's something you need to implement immediately.

CHAPTER 7

*A*hhhhh ... the customers. Ya gotta love 'em.

Seriously ... you really *do* gotta love 'em. They're like children. They're often clueless, helpless, they do stupid stuff, they piss you off ... they have to constantly be led ... they can't seem to make a decision even if their lives depend on it ... they frustrate the hell outta you.

But ya gotta love 'em. Even when you don't feel like it.

Why do you have to love 'em?, you ask.

Maybe *this* definition of a customer will help put it all into perspective:

Customer

A person who indirectly pays for all your vacations, hobbies, and golf games and gives you the opportunity to better yourself.

It's my contention, after a couple decades of observation and making this mistake myself quite a few times ... that most business owners don't love their customers sufficiently.

Or not at all.

And it's costing them an absolute frickin' fortune.

You see, my experience shows that if you truly appreciate your customer, and do some very specific and meticulously planned actions (at exactly the right times) to *show* that you appreciate him ... **you can get double, triple, or even more than triple the sales you'd normally get.**

Sound good? It *should* sound good, dummy! It's like found money ... and it costs very little to nothing to collect it.

Listen, I'm about to transform your life ... so do yourself a favor:

Turn off your IQ-lowering smart phone ...

... drag yourself away from the Internet (don't worry, the porn will still be there later) ...

... tell your spouse, children, and pets to leave you alone for the next half hour ...

... grab an adult libation of your choice ('cuz I'm *wayyyy* more entertaining when you've been imbibing) ...

... and plant your cute little *bootay* somewhere nice, comfy, and quiet so you can focus on what I'm about to impart unto you, my beloved but befuddled and bull-headed knight. (Well, you *are* stubborn at times, ya know?)

Because the stuff we're going to talk about in this chapter can be the difference between barely keeping your head above water every month, only eking out a living that provides you with a pathetic income scarcely capable of covering basic expenses ... or having a business of your dreams that gives you ...

EVERYTHING You Could Ever Possibly Desire!

Do I have your attention?

Goodie, goodie gumdrops. Then I shall *p-r-o-c-e-e-d*.

In the last chapter, in our final few minutes together, before I bid you adieu, I set the stage for this chapter by taking you back to Direct Response 101. After giving you an absolutely *brilliant* piece of direct response copy you could use to make enough money to buy a Ferrari and a 10,000-square foot house <satirical smirk>, I pontificated about how selfish and shallow your customers are, actually expecting you to send them something in return for their money.

Then I said, and I quote:

> *What you send them and how you send it can make the difference between having a thrilled customer who continues to spend money with you month after month ... or an unhappy customer who will never spend another dime with you for as long as he lives. In fact, there's a good chance he'll ask for a refund or do a chargeback.*

Don't know if you picked up on it or not but I was doing the "cliffhanger" thang, teasing you about my Master Success Formula.

You *do* want to start picking up a bunch of found money, don't you? Money you've been walking by every month, totally oblivious to the fact that it's even there? Fair enough. How about we talk about *that?*

If you want to make the maximum possible profit from each and every customer ...

What you do after the sale is just as important ... maybe even MORE important ... than what you do to get the sale in the first place!

And ... you can engineer post-sale processes and systems, triggered at exactly the right time in the customer cycle, to take advantage of some cool psychological stuff that emotionally bonds your customers to you and increases the likelihood they'll continue to spend money with you.

Pretty cool, huh?

Before I show you how I've done this (quite successfully, I might add) we need to cover some more Direct Response 101 details. What I'm about to tell you might seem obvious ... but I've never seen anybody in our little world explain it this way. Perhaps this will provide some clarity as you're figuring out how to use my Master Success Formula.

I told you what you send your customers after they send you money is important. (Duh, right?) So what should you send them?

Well, how about you send them something worth considerably less than the amount of money they paid? *Hmmmm* ... we might really be on to something here. You see, this way you get to keep most of the money. That's a good thing, right?

Now don't go getting your knickers in a bind there, Spanky. Just in case you think I'm telling you to do something dubious, dishonest, or dodgy, (I just can't help myself ... I *LOVE* alliteration) consider this:

No trader or businessperson throughout the entire course of human history has ever given equal value for equal money.

Yes, I'm even talking about all the way back to when the first caveman used a "draw on a cave wall" sales presentation (kinda like the old in-home Amway whiteboard meetings) to sell a brontosaurus meat home delivery service.

I'll say it again ... for effect. And because I need a subhead on this page ...

No Successful Salesperson Gives Equal Value for Equal Money!

To make a profit you have to sell things for more money than they're actually worth. In order to do that successfully, you have to convince the customers that the product or service is worth what they're paying.

I doubt anybody has ever explained it to you this way, but this is the basis of all marketing. When you buy anything, from a can of Coke to a Ferrari, you're paying more than the product is really worth. Otherwise, how could the manufacturer and all those middlemen make a profit?

I don't want to beat a dead horse. I'm sure you know this stuff already. But a few quick examples:

A $25,000 car costs around $7,500 to make. Those sports superstar-endorsed designer gym shoes your kids just *have* to have? The ones priced about $200? They cost about $7.50 to make. The $1,800 electric-powered leather recliner you spend way too much time in costs about $250 to make.

So what, right? Who cares? *YOU* care. At least you should. Because once you realize that no businessperson has ever given true value for the money—because it's not possible do that and make a profit—then you'll realize the fundamental truth about this crazy little direct response biz we're involved in. The truth I shall now impart unto thee, my dear knight apprentice.

The job of direct response copy is to convince your prospect that the product or service you're offering is worth the asking price. When in fact, it's worth much, much less. I guess you could dispute this and say that items are worth whatever people are prepared to pay for them . . . so any discussion of production costs and true value is meaningless.

Let's explore that for a minute. Let's say I decide to sell $10 bills online with Flakebook ads. I chose $10 bills as my product because everybody knows their real value. Ten bucks and not a penny more, right?

(Actually, it's worth NOTHING. But almost *nobody* understands that. And it would screw up my analogy. So let's just assume that they're worth 10 bucks.)

Now, lemmee see. Last I checked, my buying price for $10 bills was . . . well, $10. No matter how many I buy, I just can't seem to get a discount. Strange thing, that.

Now I have to create an ad to run on Flakebook's brilliant PPC (pay per click) ad platform to sell these brand new, crisp $10 bills. Yours, today ONLY, for just . . . *hmmmm* . . . how much should I charge?

At this point I have no idea what my CPA (cost per acquisition) will be. It all depends on about a thousand different factors, doesn't it? Let's just assume that my experience selling similar products shows that I have to allow about $8 per sale to cover the advertising costs. Great! I get to keep the remaining $2, right?

Uh, no.

I can't deliver a $10 bill digitally unless I want the Secret Service breathing down my neck . . . so I'll have shipping and handling costs. I have to pay for the envelope to send it too. Don't forget, I also have to pay my customer service people to answer calls and emails from people complaining that their $10 bill didn't arrive crisp, as promised. And all the people who want refunds. And the people who call in with questions and wind up talking for 20 minutes about their grandchildren. (I love the senior market. I really do, god bless their souls.) Yup, I gotta pay for all that too.

And then there are all sorts of other costs. The biggest being the band of criminals who threaten me with deadly force if I don't give them half of my income. Well, "criminals" was the word used in the past. Nowadays everybody just calls them "the government." So, yeah, I have to pay that cost too, I guess.

Hmmmm . . . <scratching head> . . . what else? Oh yeah . . . your credit card processor charges you a percentage of every sale. So there's that. Oh, and insurance, equipment (like computers and such) . . . and about a hundred other sundry costs that I don't feel like talking about right now.

Well, bummer. I wanted to at *least* make a profit of $2 for myself. *Hmmmm* . . . lemmee see here. Whipping it out, (my trusty calculator, that is) if I want to make a 20% profit, it looks like I have to sell these things for $50.45 each. At the very minimum. Actually, $80 is more in the ballpark.

In fact, based on my more than 20 years of experience in the direct response game, I wouldn't even begin to *think* about launching a new product if I couldn't sell it for . . .

At LEAST 8x My Cost!

And if I *really* wanted to put all the numbers in my favor for the highest possible chance of success, I should be selling these $10 bills for $100. Or more.

How many customers do you think will go for *that*? If I were a betting man I'd say absolutely none at all.

But if I were to try and sell you one of my $10 bills for $100, I could legitimately and honestly say, "*Yes, I know it's only really worth $10, but look what I had to pay to advertise it, ship it, and pay all the other costs of running a business. And I'm only taking a modest profit for all my hard work.*"

I doubt that would convince you at all to buy my $10 bill for $100, would it? You don't care what it costs to advertise and all the other costs of doing business I have to pay. You're only going to pay what the product is worth . . . $10.

But I bet you don't apply the same logic to any other item you order via direct response, do you? If I sell a product on my website for $10, I probably only paid $1 for it. This is what the item is really worth, because that's what I paid for it, right? But . . . I have to charge $10 for this $1 item because it costs me a small fortune to advertise it, pack it, ship it, handle the refunds, take care of customer service calls and emails, and make a profit. So all my marketing efforts are directed at convincing you that my product really is worth $10.

What's that you're mumbling? My disjointed diatribe about product value has bored you? You've nodded off and fallen face first into your Frosted Flakes? (They're *G-R-R-R-E-A-T!*)

Well, sit up straight, my precocious protégé and harken unto me. What we've been chitchatting about has very important implications for you if you're in any kind of business, or you're thinking about starting one. I'm trying to get you to understand one very simple fact. And although it's quite obvious, I bet it's one you've never given much thought. **It's simply this:** since you're selling products at a much higher price than they're really worth . . . usually 10 times or more . . . you're always walking on a knife's edge as far as customer satisfaction is concerned.

What's my point? There are two actually.

Point #1 is simply this:

The very best products are those for which it's difficult, if not darn near impossible, to attach any quantifiable value. By that I mean no one really knows how much the thing is worth. So your customer doesn't get upset when he receives it. My selling $10 bills analogy is the exact opposite. I think your customer will get *mightily* pissed off if he paid you $100 and you sent him a $10 bill, don't you?

That's why I think some of the very, very best products to sell via direct response marketing are info products . . . books, reports, courses, newsletters, CDs, DVDs, webinars, coaching, membership sites, etc.

Or any and all of the above delivered digitally. Why? Because these products cost very little to produce (digital versions cost *nuttin', honey,* to produce) and they're quick, cheap, and simple to fulfill.

But even more important than that . . .

Supplement Marketing Secrets

They Have an Unquantifiable Worth!

I've paid $5,000 for about 210 sheets of paper and five DVDs. The whole shootin' match probably cost less than $20 to produce. But I'm ecstatic with my purchase. Because to me, those 210 sheets of paper and five DVDs are worth exponentially more than $5,000. I've never really sat down and added it up, but I'd say, rough estimate, those 210 sheets of paper and five DVDs have been worth at least 900 times more than I paid.

And *that* is how I want your customers to feel about YOUR products too.

Moving on. Even though I didn't overtly say this in my earlier analogy,

Point #2 is this:

It ain't easy to get a new customer. And it has gotten exponentially more expensive . . . mostly thanks to the Internet lowering the barrier to entry for new businesses. So you need to do everything within your power to make your customers happy so they "stick" as long as possible, make ongoing purchases as frequently as possible, and make as many high-dollar purchases as possible.

Otherwise you'll work your ass off only to see the money go out just as fast (or faster) than it came in.

I used to say that getting a customer is like pushing a bicycle uphill . . . but getting a back end sale is like coasting downhill on that bicycle. I still use that analogy but I substitute a tricked out 967-lb Harley Davidson Hog for the bicycle. *That's* how hard it is to get a new customer nowadays in many, if not most, markets.

My opinion is biased, of course, because it's my program . . . but I think the very best way to get your customers to "stick" as long as possible, make ongoing purchases as frequently as possible and make high dollar purchases is with my . . .

Master Success Formula!

I don't see anybody talking about this stuff. And that's a sin, because I've seen this system QUADRUPLE gross sales . . . in fewer than 90 days!

I've discovered there's something I like to call the "honeymoon phase" with each new customer. It has been my experience that this phase generally lasts 90 days or less. What you do or don't do within that period mostly determines how the rest of the relationship will go with that customer.

If you do it the right way, *my* way, you'll have a customer who "sticks" a lot longer. And because of that you'll see your lifetime customer value (LCV) shoot up exponentially higher than whatever the average is for your particular niche or industry.

During this honeymoon phase, the goal is to reach out and initiate lots of positive "touches."

The goal of this program is to keep your customers happy with your company and products and build loyalty . . . so they stick around long enough to continue buying additional products and services. This is like found money . . . and it's the easiest money you'll ever make. Yet I'm constantly amazed at how few entrepreneurs understand this. And fewer still who actually implement it.

You see, I'm certain you don't want your customer acquisition to just be a "revolving door." You want long-term customers, right? If you want to enjoy the maximum profits from your business, you do.

One of the best ways to ensure you turn as many new customers as possible into long-term customers is with lots of positive touches during the honeymoon phase. The purpose of these touches is to . . .

- Show her you really care about her success with our products.
- Set her expectations about what she can expect with the use of the product(s).

- Educate him about the product he purchased. (If it was a supplement, you need to make sure he understands that natural products sometimes take a little time to start working effectively.)

- Let him know he has a "customer concierge" available at the company to answer questions, help him get the most from his purchase, coordinate the proper number of products in his monthly recurring order ... and handle any other concerns, issues, or questions. (I think customer concierge sounds way better than customer service, don't you? It conveys a Nieman Marcus image ... while customer service conveys a Walmart image in my mind.)

- Help her understand about proper use of the product(s).

- If she's on continuity, encourage her to stay on the proper amount to experience the maximum benefits.

- Help her view the recurring charge as an investment, not an expense.

A majority of these contacts during the honeymoon phase aren't to sell any additional products. They're just to reassure the customer he made a good decision, show you care, and help him understand why it's in his best interest to continue on the continuity program.

Every contact will be a low-pressure "we're just touching base to see how you're doing" kind of tone.

Here's an example of a typical honeymoon sequence:

Day 1—Step 1: As soon as possible after receiving an order (preferably the same day, or at the latest, the very next business day) **the customer will be sent, via First-Class Mail, a personalized "stick" letter.** The purpose of this letter is two-fold:

1. Prevent buyer's remorse by assuring him that he made a good decision buying your product. You do that by restating all the benefits he'll get from your product.
2. Begin to build a friendship with your customer and get him to emotionally bond with you.

To make sure this letter not only gets in the "A-pile" but it gets to the very *top* of the A-pile, I recommend you send this letter with a little theater. A low cost way to do that is by sending it in a unique envelope . . . and/or with a grabber inside so the envelope is lumpy.

My personal favorite is to send this letter on high quality Monarch stationery mailed in a matching Monarch envelope. This is how classy people used to send personal correspondence back in the day. It not only looks very upscale, but it also has a very intimate feel to it. If it's a *handwritten* letter, I've not found *anything* to rival it for intimacy.

A fancy-looking foil seal on the envelope makes sure this letter gets opened first. If you want to impart a VERY high-end feel to this letter, use a wax seal on the envelope. If I were selling a very expensive product this is what I would do. If you're not old enough to know what a wax envelope seal is, check out www.NostalgicImpressions.com/.

Day 1—Step 2: A thank-you/stick email is sent immediately after completion of the order. Whether the customer ordered online, by phone, fax, or mail you should send this email. Yes, customers still order by fax and mail. More than you probably know . . . especially if you sell to Boomers and seniors. Which I *highly* recommend you do since those are the demographics that control 70% of the discretionary income in this country.

Day 1—Step 3: Phone call #1 from the customer's concierge. This is not a sales call. It's a "welcome to the family" call. I highly doubt you'll actually *say* "welcome to the family." But that's the attitude you want to have. This might sound corny to lesser mortal marketers, but the main goal of this call is to make your customer feel loved and appreciated.

(Because tragically, almost *nobody* in his life does that. Not even his spouse or children.)

Day 1 or 2—or whenever you ship the order: **A thank-you letter goes out with the customer's order,** along with a surprise unannounced high value/low cost bonus, like a CD, DVD, special report, additional bottle of supplements, etc.

Your thank-you letter should tease about a high-value "hard" bonus your customer will get after they've been on your continuity program for six months. I gave away an MP3 player to my bodybuilding supplement auto-ship customers after they had been on the continuity six months. (Back then MP3 players had a much higher perceived value—and cost—than they do these days.) There was one condition: after six months they had to send a testimonial. It helped a lot of people stick for six months when the industry average was two months . . . and I got a lot of great testimonials.

Also include a bounce-back offer (separate from the thank-you letter) along with a discount coupon with expiration date for the product offered in the bounce-back letter.

Day 5 to 7—Or approximately one or two days after the customer's order is scheduled to arrive: auto-responder email is sent asking the customer two questions:

1. Did her order arrive OK?
2. Does she have any questions about the product?

Again, reassure her that she made a good decision and resell her on the product by painting word pictures about how she'll benefit from the product. Include your customer service phone number, website, and customer service email.

Say *WHAT?!!* You don't have customer service phone support? *Judas H. Priest!* Haven't you learned *anything* from me? Yes, it's still essential in the Internet age. In fact, if you market to Boomers and seniors, most of your customers don't even think you're a "real company" if they can't reach you by phone. Not having it is lowering your conversions too. Try it and see.

Day 10: Auto-responder with free MP3 audio, PDF report, or online bonus video. Tease about the next upcoming digital bonus.

Day 15: Phone call #2 from the customer concierge. This is a low-pressure, non-sales call. You're just checking in, making sure the customer is using the product, possibly offering ideas about how to get the best benefit from the product, etc. For supplements, if the customer's concerned because he's not seeing results, reassure him that's normal. He needs more time because natural products often take some time to "kick in." Offer a free sample of a product that works synergistically with his original product. It's an ethical bribe to keep him from dropping out of continuity.

Day 20: Auto-responder email with a back issue PDF version of the preferred customer newsletter. Tease them about the monthly customer newsletter they'll get in the mail every month for FREE, beginning next month. Build up the value of this newsletter.

We've talked about this several times in this book. The customer newsletter is a crucial element in the Master Success Formula. I've not found *anything* that makes as significant an impact in retention and boosting LCV. And believe me, I've tried to replace it with "easier" stuff, digital delivery, or even do away with it entirely. Every time I tried to do that, retention and LCV plummeted to pathetic numbers . . . essentially taking a very profitable business and deteriorating it into a revolving door business in only a couple of months.

Day 21: Customer is sent the current version of preferred customer newsletter. And it will be sent the "old skool" way . . . paper and ink via good old-fashioned snail mail. Just trust me on this. It's IMPOSSIBLE to replicate the impact of this with any form of digital delivery. I've tested it extensively. And MRI studies prove it too. Digital delivery cannot elicit the same effect in the brain chemistry. That's what makes this component so insanely effective for emotionally bonding with your customers. **THERE IS NO SUBSTITUTE FOR THIS!** So quit whining and trying to weasel out of it.

Day 23: Sales letter sent for back end product not yet purchased. And yes, it's absolutely *MANDATORY* you send this "old skool" as a direct mail letter, Doberman Dan style. The letter should include a preferred new customer discount coupon with expiration date. Yes, I realize you just sent them a newsletter a couple days ago. And you could save the postage if you include this letter with the newsletter. First of all, stop being so penny-wise and pound-foolish. We're still in the honeymoon phase, remember? We want lots of positive touches with the customer during this phase. In the future you *will* include a back end sales letter in the envelope with the monthly customer newsletter . . . but not this time.

If you think you can replace this with an email pitch, you still have a lot to learn, rookie. Direct mail was the #1 revenue generator in all my supplement businesses. The same sales copy sent in direct mail to only 3,000 customers often pulled 3x's to 4x's more orders than when it was sent by email to the entire 40,000+ customer list.

So go ahead . . . feel free to try and replace this step each month with email. I just hope you enjoy losing out on about 50% of the sales you *could* be making. And if you say *"Waaaa, waaaa, I tried it once and direct mail doesn't work for me"* then . . .

You're Doing It WRONG!

Without a doubt, the biggest bang-for-your-buck thing you could possibly do at this point in your business is figure out how to make back end direct mail work. If you can't figure it out, get in touch with me. 'Cuz I have. And it'll make you a fortune.

Day 30: Phone call #3. Another low-pressure "just checking in to see how things are going with your product" tone. You can ask them if they received the newsletter and if they liked it. If you market consumables and your customer initially only ordered a 30-day supply, you can offer her a special one-day only preferred customer deal on a multi-bottle refill order.

Day 37 to 40: Auto-responder with another free bonus delivered digitally. (MP3, PDF report, online video, etc.) Tease them about the next upcoming free bonus.

Whenever the first week of the month falls near this phase of the process: Customer receives the new issue of the customer newsletter. One of the secrets of success to your customer newsletter is consistency. I recommend sending it about five days before the first of each month. Believe me, if you think you can skip an issue . . . or send it late or haphazardly . . . you can't. Your customers will call and ask where it is. If they don't, it probably means your newsletter sucks . . . and you need to correct that post-haste. Every month you'll include at least one sales letter for a back end product with your newsletter.

Are you starting to get the rhythm of all this? Your customer newsletter goes out the first week of every month along with at least one "insert"—a back end sales letter. Once your customer list grows, as an additional source of income, you could consider selling insert space to other companies. Just make sure you always include at least one of your own in every issue.

Day 67 to 70: Auto-responder with another free bonus delivered digitally. (MP3, PDF report, online video, etc.) Tease about the next upcoming free bonus.

Day 97 to 100: Auto-responder with another free bonus delivered digitally. (MP3, PDF report, online video, etc.) Tease about next upcoming free bonus.

Day 127 to 130: Auto-responder with another free bonus delivered digitally. (MP3, PDF report, online video, etc.) Tease about the upcoming letter they will get in their snail mail in another few weeks. (See below.)

Day 165 to 170: Snail mail stick letter sent announcing the customer's upcoming six-month anniversary bonus coming next month. This is a high-perceived value "real" bonus, not a digitally delivered *thang*. In the past I've used MP3 players, leather gym bags, supplement products, info product courses (DVDs, CDs, manuals), books, toys, etc. Get creative. But it really needs to be something with a high-perceived value that will "wow" your customer. When I sent the leather gym bag, people were blown away. I think I only paid around $12 each but they were exactly like the leather bags being sold for $50 to $80 in high-end retail stores.

Listen, even if you just half-ass implement this system, it will work wonders. If you go "all in" and do this like I just showed you, it will pay off for you big time. This system took my supplement auto-ship from a pathetic one-month (or less) stick rate, and immediately bumped it up to an average of four months. That might not sound overly impressive to you . . . but it transformed my business from a "revolving door" with very little net, to a wildly profitable venture that allowed me to goof off for two whole years, only working about an hour a day to maintain things.

OK, I knew this was going to happen. I can hear what you're thinking: *"This all sounds good, Dan. But gee whiz whillikers . . . I don't have the time or the money to do all this."* Look, rookie . . . I ran the numbers and here's what I found:

You Can't Afford to NOT Do This!

Look, the costs of doing this are marginal. But the costs of *not* doing this are much greater than you can possibly imagine. After all, customer acquisition costs are as high as I've ever seen them. You're probably spending more and more each month to get new customers. Doesn't it make sense to extract every penny of profit possible? And you're also making your customer as happy as possible. It's win/win. I see no downside at all. OK, so let's talk turkey. How much does it cost to do all this?

I've seen some BIG results from the Master Success Formula. How much? How does a 2x bump in NET in only a few months sound? Yeah ... *that* good. This is something you need to implement immediately.

In the next chapter, I'm going to reveal some customer service tweaks that can produce EXPONENTIAL boosts in sales. It's like found money.

CHAPTER 8

Here's what we're going to talk about in this chapter. There's nothing more profitable you could possibly do for your business. Without a doubt it is . . .

The "Lowest Hanging Fruit" and Highest ROI Activity You Can Invest In!

With the exception of a very interesting entrepreneur I recently met, in my 21 years of marketing experience, I really haven't seen *any* businesses do much of anything to maximize their profitability from their existing customers.

They all just focus on the *getting* of new customers. Love 'em and leave 'em. Wham, bam, thank you, ma'am. Then the thrill is gone . . . the chase is over . . . the prey has been captured. Time to move on to the next target.

Sure, a few companies constantly pitch back end products (which I highly endorse) but almost nobody strategically engineers a system to get their customers to stick for as long as possible.

And that's sad . . . because these entrepreneurs are clueless about how much money they're losing without this plan. In my case, the program I shared with you in this book 4x'd my gross sales and continuity retention in only about a three-month period. Over time it got even better.

That was *life changing* for me. It freed me . . . figuratively and literally. I was no longer stuck working nonstop in the business, grinding it out day after day. My profit margin was so damn high I was able to put the whole kit and caboodle on auto-pilot while I pretended like I was a real musician for two years.

Wanna know *why* my profit margin was so high? (You ask easy questions.) Because . . .

A Back End Sale Is the Lowest Cost— Yet Highest Profit Sale You'll Ever Make!

When your "stick" program is running like a finely tuned Swiss watch, your back end sales come in like clockwork.

Doesn't it just make sense to get a lot more out of what you've already got? You can't lower your customer acquisition costs to increase profits. In fact, that's a really dumb move. (Actually, you probably should be spending as much as possible to acquire a new customer.) So it just makes sense to get more profit from each customer.

That's why I get so frustrated and simply don't understand why I have to sell this program so frickin' hard to most entrepreneurs. They seem to *like* having a Casanova love 'em and leave 'em/revolving door business instead of a long-term, auto-pilot, money-printing machine.

I just don't get it. Must be a self-sabotage/fear of prosperity issue.

Damaging Admission

Admittedly, with my *Marketing Camelot*, I'm only doing a portion of the program I outlined in this book. (With a couple of cool little "neurological anchoring" twists I added.) But even just doing a *part* of it, I currently have 8x longer retention over the industry average for programs priced at less than *half* of mine.

Anyhoo . . . since you read that last chapter, I bet you've been coming up with a big long list of excuses as to why you can't implement my strategies.

So you like to make excuses, do ya? Well here's what I say to that:

We Excuse Our Sloth under the Pretext of Difficulty

OK, you caught me. It's not a Doberman Dan quote. But it's what I *would* have said if Marcus Fabius Quintilian hadn't beaten me to the punch several thousand years ago. I just would've said it in a much less eloquent and cruder, street-like manner.

If one of your excuses is cost, allow me to shoot that one down right now.

Step #1

Remember this one? One of the most important steps, based on my experience. Just in case, a brief refresher:

> *As soon as possible after receiving an order (preferably the same day, or at the latest, the very next business day) the customer will be sent, via First-Class Mail, a personalized "stick letter."*

I'm currently using *high-quality Monarch stationery mailed in a matching Monarch envelope with foil seal.*

See this link: www.AmericanStationery.com

I order the ivory sheets because it looks classier than white. You can get a box of 100 sheets for $9.95 (2015 price).

And I get the Monarch envelopes here: www.Amazon.com/MonarchEnvelopes

A box of 100 goes for $9.95 (2015 price).

The purpose of this personalized letter is to make a positive impact using a little "theater." With the style of stationery, little used (nowadays) Monarch size, font choice, and personalization, the goal is to convey that you appreciate and care enough about the customers to personally acknowledge their order.

Almost NOBODY sends a personal letter sealed with a foil seal anymore. This style of stick letter has made quite an impact in two different businesses of mine. Aside from me, I've never seen ANYBODY use this style and format for a stick letter.

With the personal "A-pile" look, this letter stands a very high chance of getting opened immediately and read.

Step #1 Costs

- Approximately 19 cents for the stationery and matching envelope
- As of the time of this writing, a First-Class stamp is a mere 49 cents
- **Total:** 68 cents

One hundred of these letters can be quickly and easily merged/personalized on a laser printer in 10 minutes or less. The only other cost is folding, inserting, and placing a stamp on the envelope. I have no idea how to estimate your employee costs for that. I guess that depends on how much you pay your employees.

Or you can go with the "no employees" plan like me and have McMannis Duplication and Fulfillment do it for you. That's definitely the most efficient way I've ever done it . . . and it's fairly darn affordable too.

You can contact the fine folks at McMannis here: www.McMannisInc.com.

Let's move on to . . .

Step #2

Remember this one? Within one to two days of shipping the order, the customers should receive a phone call from their customer "concierge."

This isn't a sales call. It's a "stick" call to prevent buyer's remorse by reassuring the customers that they made a wise decision in purchasing your product. It's also to educate and explain how to best use the product for maximum benefits and answer any questions, etc.

Yes, the primary intention of this call isn't to sell anything. But it often leads to back end sales if the concierge finds it appropriate to suggest other products that can help, based on what the customer says.

If at all possible, it's preferable to have a woman make these calls. Forgive me if this sounds sexist, but I've found both men and women react much more favorably to receiving a phone call like this from a woman. When the call is made by a friendly woman with a pleasant phone manner, the customers are usually much more polite than they would be with a man. It also appears that most customers feel less pressured and they don't react negatively like many people react to telemarketers.

Your concierge should have sufficient people skills/persuasion skills to go with the flow and improvise, because every call is going to be a little different.

It's a really good idea to provide each concierge with access to some kind of customer contact management system to record notes about the conversation. Stuff like health issues mentioned by the customer and personal details like their dog's name. (I'm not kidding!) And any other personal and relationship-building details that can be referred to on follow-up calls.

Step #2 Costs

I can only guesstimate the time involved in each call could be anywhere from 15 seconds if the customer doesn't answer . . . and up to 10 to 15 minutes if the customer has a lot of questions or is particularly chatty. That's often the case with Boomers and seniors.

Ideally, for ALL these concierge calls we would like to talk to the customer instead of leaving a message. That more than likely means these calls will need to be made in the evenings. You can do this in-house or outsource it.

Hmmmm . . . what other costs do we need to speak about? Oh yeah, I remember . . .

Monthly Newsletter Costs

Publishing a newsletter is a topic worthy of having an entire book. Actually it would take a *series* of books to cover everything about the topic. On second thought, to really do it justice, I'd need to create an entire course.

Maybe one day.

Until then, let me share what almost everybody asks me about publishing a customer newsletter:

How much does it cost? (Cost is almost always the #1 or #2 excuse given for not creating and sending a newsletter. You'll soon see that excuse doesn't hold water.)

IMPORTANT

These monthly newsletters should NOT be stuffed in the box with the customer's monthly continuity shipment or regular order. They need to be mailed separately from the product, preferably no later than the first week of the month. For a couple reasons:

1. We're positioning this newsletter as a high-value bonus they get from being a preferred customer and/or continuity member. Therefore, the fulfillment and quality of the newsletter must be congruent with that image.

2. Sending the newsletter separately from the monthly product shipment adds one additional positive contact the customer has with us each month. And, if you remember from previous conversations in this book, the more positive "touches" the customers get from us each month—*especially* during the "honeymoon phase"—the longer their stick rate and higher the LCV.

Time to talk turkey. (Man, that's an old idiom. First recorded use was 1824, if you care to know. It's a saying the Native Americans used during one of the countless instances when white guys were trying to screw them and rob them blind. Useless trivia, I know. But still kinda interesting.)

Printing and postage depends on the length of the newsletter. For this example, let's assume it's a B&W, four-pager, printed on 11x17, and booklet folded to 8 ½ x 11, then trifolded and inserted into a #10 envelope.

- Printing—approx. 5 to 10 cents
- Lettershop services (printing envelopes, inserting, sealing, applying postage, and delivery to USPS)—approximately 30 cents
- First-Class postage—49 cents (pre-sorted standard could drop it to about 30 cents.)
- Total approximate costs: (If mailed First Class) 84 to 89 cents.

Yeah, 89 measly cents. *That* is what's keeping you from doing it? Something relatively hassle free and simple that could double . . . triple . . . quadruple . . . or *more!* . . . your customer retention?

Look, if you ignore this, you forfeit any right to bitch about profits, acquisition costs, sucky continuity retention, or any of the other "revolving door" problems I'm sure you're gonna have in the future. **This one thing is one of my biggest secrets to bumping up your LCV higher than all your competitors and making a LOT more money from your present business.**

Judas H. Priest on a pogo stick! You can be one big burly bull-headed bastard sometimes, ya know that? (Yeah, I could hear the excuses you were making inside that pretty little melon of yours.) Look, I have no reason to lie to you. This one thing—just the simple addition of a free monthly customer newsletter . . .

QUADRUPLED Retention in My Continuity Program!

You can't even imagine what that did to my bottom line. My life improved *dramatically* in only about four months. And I ain't exactly the brightest crayon in the box. I did a bunch of stuff wrong. Imagine what it could it do for you if you listened to me and did everything *right*?

I grow weary of this. (Spoken in my best aristocratic English accent.) Let me wrap this up so I can get into something else that will help you mine a big ole heaping pile o' gold hidden in your business.

Other Costs

What else is left? Oh yeah, you're sending out a series of carefully timed auto-responder messages with free bonuses of cool digital products. Tap, tap, tapping away on my trusty adding machine with hand crank, it appears the cost to do this adds up to . . .

Nuttin' Honey!

(I often wonder if my pop culture references are lost on my younger knights. Whatever. They amuse *me* and that's all that matters.)

Moving on.

The only other step in the sequence that really has a cost is the six-month anniversary reward gift. What you give them will probably depend on the price point of your product and profit margins. If you're selling fractional ownership in a Lear Jet, you're gonna look like a penny-pinching cheap bastard if you give them a $2 knick-knack. You really should gift them something with a commensurate value to the level of clientele you're working with. If you sell a $40 bottle of pills, you're not going to give them a Mont Blanc Meisterstück 90th Anniversary Special Edition pen. (Although that would be a good gift for your private jet clients.)

Look, I've got several variations of my Master Success Formula with different steps and sequences, depending on the business. What I have told you is the tried and true basic formula . . . and it flat out works like Viagra on steroids. You can just use that as is and you'll do extremely well.

CHAPTER 9

A Bonus

In keeping with our "get more out of what you've already got" theme, allow me to share some more simple, yet highly effective ways you can beef up your back end and boost your bottom line. (Alliteration *rules*, dude!)

Working with my supplement business coaching protégés, and now with my own recently launched supplement business, I've had a lot of opportunities to study the different things a good call center can do for your business.

I've also seen what a mediocre and bad call center will do to your business and the relationship with your customer.

This one aspect of your business can be the difference between you having a "churn 'em and burn 'em" daily grind j-o-b ... or ...

An Insanely Profitable "Print Money at Will" Machine!

Even though very few entrepreneurs do it, I've seen what using outbound customer service calls can do for your bottom line. It's a proven profit center for most businesses. But I met a dude who has taken my concept to an *entirely* different level. And it's producing extraordinary boosts in back end sales, continuity retention, and lifetime customer value (LCV).

Allow me to introduce you to Chris Daigle and his very successful venture, Federated Phone Systems.

As with most entrepreneurial ventures, this one came about almost completely by accident.

It all started when Chris launched a fairly aggressive direct mail campaign. Chris has mailed millions of pieces of direct mail. He told me he likes direct mail because you can do business in a vacuum. (A man after my own heart.) If you've ever had anybody knock off your successful online promo or entire online business, I'm sure you can appreciate that. It's hard for people to rip off your website when there *is* no website.

So direct mail was generating lots of inbound calls for Chris. That's a *good* thing, right? Well, yes and no. It's good to have lots of calls. But it's bad when they're outsourced to an unscrupulous and/or incompetent or lackadaisical call center. (And there are a *lot* of those.)

Rather than spend weeks (or in some cases, months) vetting call centers, like a true entrepreneur, Chris decided to start his own in-house call center.

Things were going along just swimmingly with this arrangement. He could train his phone people in exactly the way he wanted them to treat the callers, what they say, the order in which they say it, what they offer, handling objections, etc. And more important, he could supervise them to make sure they're doing what he trained them to do.

Then He Had a Crazy Idea . . .

What if he used this business as a platform to not only improve his customers' lives, but improve his team members' lives too? Of course, they would get a paycheck . . . and he would also reward them based on performance . . . but what if he provided them more?

What if he created the most positive and supportive atmosphere possible? And what if he provided regular training? Yes, sales training, of course. (Duh, right?) But what if he took it further? What if he showed them how what they're doing is changing people's lives? Show them the bigger picture? Get them out of the "we're just hawking a bottle of pills" mentality and show them how lives are being changed by these products?

And what if he exposed them to training showing how to realize and maximize their full potential? What if he gave them access to materials that could help them grow and become the person they were born to be.

He thought, *"What if I could do that? What impact would it have on our customers? My team members? Gee . . . what impact would that have on the entire frickin'* **WORLD?**

"And I bet, as a nice little serendipity, I'd see some huge leaps in my bottom line numbers too.

"Geez, I can't see any downside to doing this!"

Quite honestly, I don't know if those were the *exact* thoughts Chris had at the time . . . but it's what I'm imagining he thought.

What came of his crazy idea? Results were spectacular. Better than anybody expected.

I guess Chris just couldn't keep a good thing to himself. He mentioned how well his little experiment was working out to a few of his entrepreneur buddies. What happened next is not surprising in the least.

A friend who has a very successful supplement company reached out and said, *"Hey, old buddy, old pal. Could we maybe use your phone peeps to do a couple of experiments of our own?"*

Our hero (Chris) said, *"Absolutely man. You run a very clean business, your supplements are super high grade, and you're not doing too badly in the sales department either. I think if we help you, you could be doing **much** better."*

(At the time this guy's supplement biz was doing about $3 million a month in sales.)

His friend (and now new client) said, *"I just want you to call and reach out to my customers. There's a lot of noise on the Internet. We're getting refund requests for supplements that we don't even sell. There seems to be a lot of confusion in the marketplace. If you could just reach out to my customers after they buy, let them know their order's on the way and let them know they bought from a real company . . . I think we'd see some good results from that."*

Wanna know what that sounds like to me?

Easy Money!

Doesn't it? Use your agents' down time when they're not taking inbound calls to make a few outbound calls for another business? Time they would have normally spent twiddling their thumbs. Or more likely, texting their friends . . . or looking at pictures of animals on Facebook.

So Chris diverted some of his agents' time, when they weren't taking inbound calls, to doing some outbound calls for his friend. It wasn't really sophisticated. All they did was call and welcome the customer, confirm the order and tell him or her how to get in touch with customer service if they had any questions or needed anything. That's it.

What his client noticed was fairly amazing. His refund rate dropped significantly. And they hadn't changed anything except adding these outbound calls. It saved a couple hundred thousand dollars a month in refunds.

Chris thought to himself, *"Wow, maybe this outbound call thang is going to work."* (I highly doubt Chris used the word thang. That's actually *my* thang. But this was the first opportunity I've had to use it in this chapter.)

Chris and his friend started brainstorming. They said, *"Why don't we transition these welcome calls into an opportunity to explore other health concerns the customers have? And if it's something that other products would help, we'll tell them about a special offer going on. We can include a joint relief product, heart health product, probiotic . . . whatever they need . . . and create a special package for them."*

From day one it was a . . .

Smashing Success!

This isn't some kind of *Wolf of Wall Street* boiler room vibe. Quite the opposite. Chris only hires customer service agents with excellent people skills. People who are very comfortable on the phone and have great telephone voices . . . but they're *not* sales people.

What Chris did was really dive deep into the customer mindset. What are they thinking? What are they feeling? What are they worried about? What are they most skeptical about? Then he tried to figure out why they don't take the products . . . why they don't get results (mostly because they don't take the product) . . . and why they request a refund.

He wanted to figure out how his friend/client could keep these people around longer. If they could just get *one* additional order from these customers over and above the current average reorder rate, it would have a HUGE effect on the bottom line.

So they did a test. They didn't want this to be an aggressive sales call. They wanted it to be a comfortable and friendly call that didn't leave people feeling like they had been attacked by a phone shark.

There was a lot of experimentation with scripting . . . and continuous tweaking of those scripts based on the customers' reactions and results.

There was constant quality assurance going on and supervision of the agents. They listened to all the calls to see how their plan was working.

Long story short, the client started making money with nearly every single activity they did with these customer assurance calls. Sales of his entire supplement line immediately jumped up.

Most supplement buyers are Boomers and seniors. And contrary to what most lesser mortal marketers think, there are a lot of people in those demographics who are still not Internet savvy. There are quite a lot of them who don't buy online and very rarely even use the Internet.

So that's the mindset you're dealing with for a lot of supplement customers. Getting a phone call from a company they just did business with was *extremely* well received because lesser mortal marketers *never* do it.

People were saying things like, *"Wow, nobody has ever called me before. This is great. Thank you for checking in with me."* And the biggie . . .

"It's So Nice to Do Business with a Real Company."

I made that last sentence a subhead because this is a key ingredient most online business owners are missing. And it's costing them a fortune.

The agent reinforced that the customer had made the right buying decision because, hey . . . this is a "real company." They also restated some of the benefits of the product and asked if they had any questions. They also told the customer how to contact them by phone if they had any questions or needed help with anything. All this was meticulously engineered to prevent buyer's remorse.

The customers loved the fact that they didn't have to send an email or support ticket and wait 36 to 48 hours for some lame boilerplate cut-

and-paste customer service response. They can simply do what's in their comfort zone . . . an activity they have grown up with . . .

Pick Up the Phone and Call!

Just so you're clear on this, what we're talking about is *outbound* calling. Yup, that old "outdated" activity that strikes fear into the hearts of many marketers. Well, at least the marketers who haven't done their homework and their learnin' only goes as far back as the Internet Marketing gurus. (Damn rookies.)

There are plenty of companies that take inbound calls but very few who specialize in outbound calling. Well, to be more accurate, there are very few who specialize in outbound calling and know how to do it right.

And that's a shame, because when done the right way— the way I'm about to show you—it can be one of your . . .

Biggest and Most Consistent Sales Generators!

Boy, oh boy. If somebody smart decided to listen to me and combine this little outbound calling secret with direct mail . . . you could most likely have one of the fastest, if not *THE* fastest growing business in your market.

And even more important, should the idea of cashing out and cruising the world on your own yacht appeal to you, you could sell a business with these two components in place (direct mail and an outbound calling system) for a multiple of 3x, 4x, or even 5x more than all your competitors who are too stupid or lazy (or both) to do it.

Is there a catch? Yeah, kinda. When taking inbound calls, your agents don't really need to be all that great on the phone. It helps if they are but don't count on that. (There's a lot of employee turnover in that biz.) All they really have to be good at is sticking to the script. And it would be nice if they read it like they had a personality too.

See, with inbound calls, your customer is picking up the phone to call YOU. They've already seen your sales copy and they know what supplement they have in mind and are already highly predisposed to ordering. For age, culture, and demographic reasons they feel more comfortable ordering over the telephone. They are in their comfort zone. You really don't have to be a salesperson to complete that transaction.

Outbound calling is a completely different animal. *YOU* are calling *THEM*. That immediately changes the climate of things. The barriers are immediately up. Initially at least. And that's the first obstacle you need to overcome.

Yes, I know this ain't a sexy online BSO (bright shiny object) and it actually involves a little work <gulp!> setting it up. But for your sake, I seriously hope you keep an open mind because, if your experience is like mine and many other veteran marketers, you'll find that this little gem of a marketing idea could very well . . .

Eclipse Everything You've Ever Done!

Yes, I realize it's probably not your core competency. Most of us introverted, hide-behind-a-keyboard copywriters and online marketers started a direct response business so we don't have to talk to anybody. I get it. I really do.

But never fear. I've got your back. I'm going to explain this complete system. I'll show you the tools you need to implement it in your business, how the calls should go, what should and shouldn't be said . . . everything. You're also probably going to experience a paradigm shift about scripts. It's quite contrarian to what most people think. And the thing I'm *sure* you'll be excited to hear is . . .

You Personally Do Not Have to Make the Calls!

(I swear I just heard a collective "whew.") If you have a staff in place . . . or even if you want to try it yourself . . . I'm going to give you everything you need to get this off the ground. And if you prefer the 100% hands-off option, I'll show you the very best way I know to farm it all out and still get excellent results.

You could implement this system in just a few days and start seeing a substantial ROI in less than a week. It ain't exactly rocket surgery. But there are a few critical tweaks you gotta get right and pitfalls you must avoid. If you don't know these, you'll just be spinning your wheels.

Whoops, we're out of pages in this book. But don't worry. I reveal all the details about this big money generating call system to my knights in the *Marketing Camelot*. If you're already a knight (subscriber), you'll be able to get updates. If not, what are you waiting for?

http://MarketingCamelot.com/

Pax vobiscum.

ABOUT THE AUTHOR

Doberman Dan is a 30-year serial entrepreneur and direct response copywriter.

He has worked in a variety of niches but his specialty has been the health, fitness and bodybuilding markets.

Dan has started and built 3 of his own supplement businesses and sold two of them, enjoying two different bouts of mini-retirement.

He has recently been hired by a $600 million/year company to help them start a brand new supplement division.

He has been publishing *The Doberman Dan Letter* at http://MarketingCamelot.com since 2011 and has many of the most successful direct marketers in the world as subscribers.

Dan has written hundreds of successful ads, direct mail packages, websites, e-mail marketing campaigns, feature articles, and newsletters.

His ads and articles have appeared in…

- Entrepreneur
- Investors Business Daily

- Penthouse
- MuscleMag International
- Flex
- Muscle & Fitness
- Men's Edge
- IronMan
- Muscular Development
- Reps!
- Exercise For Men Only
- Natural Bodybuilding & Fitness
- The National Enquirer
- Weekly World News
- And numerous mainstream newspapers and magazines.

Over the course of his marketing and copywriting career Dan has seen the same mistakes repeated over and over again by most supplement business owners.

He has consistently doubled, tripled, and sometimes more than quadrupled sales and profits for supplement businesses within only a few months with his unique and proven approach to advertising and marketing.

He shares some of these ideas for building your business and increasing your profits for free online.

These secrets can send your sales and profits soaring… faster than you ever imagined. They can radically change your income and your entire life in practically no time at all.

You can find more info about the author, along with more than 200 FREE articles about successful marketing at…

http://DobermanDan.com

Made in the USA
Columbia, SC
05 March 2021